INTRODUCTION TO THE STUDY OF DOGMATICS

Hendrikus Berkhof

Translated by
John Vriend

WILLIAM B. EERDMANS PUBLISHING COMPANY
GRAND RAPIDS, MICHIGAN

Copyright © 1985 by William B. Eerdmans Publishing Company
255 Jefferson Ave. S.E., Grand Rapids, Mich. 49503

Translated from the Dutch edition, *Inleiding tot de studie van de Dogmatiek,*
© Uitgeversmaatschappij J. H. Kok — Kampen 1982

Library of Congress Cataloging-in-Publication Data

Berkhof, H. (Hendrikus), 1914-
  Introduction to the study of dogmatics.

  1. Theology, Doctrinal — Introductions. I. Title.
BT65.B47 1985   230   85-15979

ISBN 0-8028-0045-9

CONTENTS

71582

CONTENTS

One

AN INTRODUCTION
THAT AIMS TO INITIATE

Numerous books, both large and small, have been written as introductions to a specific field of study. But they do not always have the same aim by far. Some treat the basic problems of a given field and their solutions as the author sees them. They assume that the readers are already well initiated in the subject matter. What they offer is the product of long study and is intended as an insightful summary. One has to be in the field a fairly long time to be able to profit from it. Sometimes these introductions read as if they were written for colleagues in the field in order to offer a personal viewpoint as an addition or alternative to theirs.

This little book belongs to a second sort of introduction. It literally seeks to be an intro-duction. That is, it aims to put into the hands of young students, just beginning their study of dogmatics, a first initiation. It is not so much a summary, therefore, as a collection of points of entry. It does not get beyond the fragmentary. It is a map of the country as a whole offered in the hope that acquaintance with it will induce the reader to travel there. But, however modest, it seeks to be an initiation. After reading it the reader should know what to expect of the field—no more, no less.

These last words acquire their own weight in the study of

dogmatics. For among theological students this discipline exerts both a strong repulsive and a strong attractive force. It tends to evoke very contradictory feelings: curiosity, enthusiasm, fear, aversion. There is an awareness that to a high degree one hazards his or her own self when beginning the study of this discipline. Some have begun to study theology precisely in order to get to this field: they expect from it a deepening and clarifying of their own faith, and an answer to questions concerning the truth of God and the meaning of life, questions that torment them. Some, on the other hand, are afraid that it will spoil their faith: you are wrong to want to approach such large subjects systematically and intellectually. Faith loses its spontaneity and openness if you do. Still others are afraid that systematic reflection will undermine the faith: did not Jesus say that it is hidden from the wise and learned but revealed to little children? To raise questions is to raise doubts. One is better off not to want to think things through too far. Still others fear the opposite, that this discipline might force them to make personal decisions that they are at pains to keep at arms' length by a quiet, "objective," theological practice.

It is my hope as author that all these students will be able after a while to determine their attitude toward this threatening, yet fascinating, field of study with a greater degree of awareness.

Finally, three more remarks of a more material nature:

1. In 1973 I wrote a dogmatics of my own. That may be a disadvantage, for before I am aware of it I may be ventilating my own ideas under the guise of an impartial introduction. I wish to assure my readers that in writing this volume I constantly kept this danger in mind. And it proved to me to be a source of fascination that such an introduction had to meet a very different set of criteria from those that apply to dogmatics itself. The question is whether or not I succeeded . . . ; that, the reader will have to judge.

2. I am a Protestant in the Reformed tradition. That will, of course, be noticeable throughout. But it will also be clear, I hope, that I have followed other types of dogmatics, post – Vatican II Roman Catholic theology in particular, with great attentiveness. I would very much like to see that precisely this kind of introduction would prove useful at a variety of

theological institutions. That could only favor the hoped-for and already emerging convergence of dogmatic methods and pro-nouncements — something that is, in addition, of the highest ecu-menical importance.

3. The feminist movement has sensitized me to the issue of sexist language. For that reason I regret that in this book I had to speak of the dogmatician over and over as "he," while I am personally acquainted with a growing number of gifted woman dogmaticians. But to do otherwise would make the style just too artificial. So let us agree: "he" means "he and/or she"!

Two

NAME AND CONCEPT

2.1 DOGMA

Words ending in *-ics* (e.g., ethics, hermeneutics, liturgics, pedagogics) refer to a scientific discipline, and specifically that discipline whose field of study is indicated by the preceding syllable(s). Dogmatics, then, is the scientific study of dogma.

But what is this "dogma"? *Dogma* is a Greek word, referring to what seems correct to a person, that which that person sets forth as his conviction. It was used in philosophy, with reference to philosophic doctrines, and in politics, with reference to decisions and edicts of a government. Both meanings occur in the New Testament, the first in Ephesians 2:15 and Colossians 2:14 and 20, the second in Luke 2:1 and Acts 17:7. It is clear from the first use that the word could have the unfavorable connotation of false teachings. But in the church the positive meaning gained the upper hand: the true doctrine, that is, the truth revealed by God in Christ and Scripture (later it also came to be seen as revealed in church tradition). The gatherings of the bishops of the entire church, called councils, which began in 325 (at Nicea), strove diligently to formulate that truth clearly over against the errors of heretics. These pronouncements, which were considered authoritative, were designated especially, and

4

collectively, as "dogma." After the end of the fourth century the emperors also proclaimed them as decrees of the state. From that time on (into the eighteenth century!) both original meanings therefore coincided.

In the early church, seven of such dogma-producing councils were held, the first in 325 and the last in 787. They attempted to define the true doctrine concerning Christ, his relationship to God, and his two natures (divine and human); and in that context also the doctrine concerning the Holy Spirit and the Trinity. The Eastern church (the church of Greece, the Balkan countries, the Near East, and Russia) had no other councils after these seven and therefore proclaimed no additional new dogmas. The Western church, under the leadership of the pope, believed it could convene councils without the participation of the East. A number of them met to define dogmas, notably the Fourth Lateran Council (1215; the doctrine of transubstantiation), the Council of Trent (1545–1563; the doctrines of Scripture and tradition, grace and free will, and the sacraments and the sacrifice of the mass), and the First Vatican Council (1869–1870; the relationship between faith and reason, and the infallibility of the pope). Since then a pope has also proclaimed a dogma without convening a council, that is, the doctrine of the bodily Assumption of Mary (November 1, 1950). Thus there are, certainly in the Roman Catholic Church, a fair number of dogmas, though far fewer than outsiders often think: an assortment of pronouncements and decrees handed down by councils and popes, however weighty, still do not claim to be dogmas; that is, they do not presume to give infallible expression to revealed truth.

From the above it has already become clear why Protestant churches have produced no dogmas. For them the infallible authority of the Bible is above that of the fallible church. Article VII of the Belgic Confession says, for example, "Neither may we compare any writings of men, though ever so holy, with those divine Scriptures . . . nor councils, decrees, or statutes." In the churches of the Reformation, confessions of faith take the place of dogmas. In the phrase "confessions of faith" one clearly detects a subjective element. These documents are therefore in principle open to correction (as has actually happened in the case of the Belgic Confession). Besides, the Reformation churches were organized in terms of national boundaries and were also rather different among themselves. In that framework a general council could take place only with difficulty. Only the Synod of Dordt (1618–1619) remotely resembled a council, just as its canons remotely resemble a body of dogma. All this does not mean that Protestant churches rejected all dogmas proclaimed earlier. Medieval and later dogmas were rejected *in toto,* but earlier ones, certainly those of the fourth and the fifth centuries, were regarded as scriptural and were mentioned as such in Protestant creeds.

2.2 DOGMATICS

After the preceding discussion one might think that something like dogmatics can exist only in the Roman Catholic Church and to a lesser extent in the Eastern Orthodox Church, and that Protestant churches must have completely dispensed with both the name and the content of dogmatics. But the opposite is the case. The name, rather, is a Protestant invention, probably coined by the German theologian L. Fr. Reinhart, who in 1659 published a book under the title *Synopsis theologiae dogmaticae.* But in that work he did not deal with all existing dogmas and he certainly did not deal only with dogmas. Before him, also, there was really no discipline that limited itself to dogmas. Dogmatics in the strict sense had never existed as a separate discipline. People wrote books about the main components of the Christian faith, books in which at fixed points certain dogmas were explained, but in the Latin of those ages such books were called *compendium, enchiridion, expositio, institutio, loci, medulla, sententiae, summa, syntagma,* or *theologia.* I have not been able to find out why Reinhart added the word *dogmatica* to this collection (perhaps he used it to distinguish his work from a pure *theologia biblica*). What is certain is that in time this name gained almost exclusive acceptance.

2.3 DOGMATICS OR DOCTRINE OF FAITH?

One may regret that the discipline under discussion is referred to so incompletely and inadequately as "dogmatics." This is the more so because in general usage the adjective "dogmatic" and the noun "dogmatism" are so reminiscent of the authoritarian church in which dogmas originated and developed, with the connotation of "imposing unproven assertions." This is not what characterizes the discipline that grew historically under an assortment of names, not even in the Roman Catholic tradition. (For that matter it may perhaps be a telling thing that Pope John XXIII, with the agreement of very many others, proclaimed the Second Vatican Council as a "pastoral" council that would for once not announce any dogmas.) The name "dogmatics" would fit better as a designation for what is usually called "symbolics," the field of study in which the material of dogmas and of the creeds of the churches is set forth in an orderly but descriptive fashion. A normative discipline like "dogmatics" deserves another and clearer name.

Such a name surfaced a century after the appearance of the name "dogmatics." In 1759 and 1760, S. J. Baumgarten published his dogmatics under the title *Evangelische Glaubenslehre* (the evangelical doctrine of faith). Later, after the appearance of Schleiermacher's dogmatics under the name *Der christliche Glaube* (1821), many adopted that designation. At the same time, as a consequence, the name given to this field of study became a plaything in the struggle between left and right in the churches. For the left, "dogmatics" was too objective and authoritarian; for the right, "doctrine of faith" was too subjective and relativizing. The latter, however, may not at all be the case: "faith" is a biblical concept, meaning an act of surrender, and implying a truth outside and above us. Nowadays the difference between the two will not be felt so strongly. But "dogmatics" held the day, especially because this name had become a part of university parlance, at least in several European countries. In the Anglo-Saxon world people speak of "systematic theology" or even simply of "theology." Attempts to introduce the name "systematic theology" in the Netherlands have not been successful because it was said that the philosophy of religion and ethics would also fall under that heading.

2.4 CONCEPT AND DEFINITION

In the meantime we must not for the sake of problems associated with the name forget the matter itself. It is getting high time to indicate somewhat more clearly what it is we are to think on meeting that—perhaps—infelicitous name. The concept is more important than the name. We will get nearest the matter itself if we try to define it. But for every dogmatician there is a different definition. So we shall first list a few definitions.

Thomas Aquinas speaks of dogmatics as teaching "on God as principal and on creatures in relation to him, who is their origin and end" (*Summa Theologica,* I.1.3.i [Blackfriars, 1964]). The seventeenth-century Lutheran Hollaz defines it as "the doctrine concerning God, which teaches man, from the divine Word, as to the true method of worshiping God in Christ unto eternal life" (quoted in Heinrich Schmid, *The Doctrinal Theology of the Evangelical Lutheran Church,* 3d ed., trans. Hay and Jacobs [Augsburg, 1961], p. 16). The seventeenth-century Reformed theologian Johann Heinrich Heidegger speaks at somewhat greater length of "the doctrine of God reconciling man the sinner to Himself in Christ and duly to be known of him and worshipped in godly-wise, a doctrine taught of God who reveals it by His Word, and purely instituted as in His presence for man the sinner's salvation and for the glory of God's name" (Heidegger, I.14, as quoted in Heinrich Heppe's *Reformed Dogmatics,* Thomson translation, p. 10). Very different indeed is the definition of Schleiermacher, who calls dogmatics "the science which systematizes the doctrine prevalent in a Christian Church at a given time" (*The Christian Faith* [MacIntosh and Stewart, 1928], p. 88).

In the second half of the nineteenth century we hear the Lutheran J. Chr. K. von Hofmann describe dogmatics as "the exposition of the simple facts which makes the Christian a Christian and distinguishes him from a non-Christian, in order to set forth the manifold riches of its content" (*Der Schriftbeweis,* 1:10-12, passim). Herman Bavinck describes dogmatics as "the scientific system of the knowledge of God which he has revealed to the church in his Word . . . a knowledge concerning himself and all creatures as standing in relation to him" (*Gereformeerde Dogmatiek,* 1:15). Karl Barth opens his *Church Dogmatics* with the proposition: "As a theological discipline dogmatics is the scientific self-examination of the Christian Church with respect to the content of its distinctive talk about God" (I/1, 1). The present-day Roman Catholic dogmatician Karl Rahner says it is "a science of faith, a reflexive, methodical, systematic grasp, by the believer in the light of faith, of the salvific self-disclosure of the Triune God in Christ and the Church as his body" (Rahner, Vorgrimler, *Theological Dictionary* [Herder and Herder, 1965], p. 135). The author of the present volume prefers to speak of dogmatics as "systematic and thorough reflection on the content of the relationship which God has established with us in Christ."

This small anthology already points to a wide divergence in method. Is God himself the object of this study? Or is it, more indirectly, the knowledge of his revelation? And do we know that revelation from the Bible, or in Christ, or from the church, or from the history of dogma, or from the preaching of the church? Or is the reflection of the individual on his own faith pivotal? In the definitions themselves profound dogmatic differences already come to the surface. Still, we must not exaggerate these differences. No one will deny that Christ, the Bible, the church, and the Spirit-renewed human being all cohere and form parts of one redemptive process. Even when a person enters this complex of redemptive happenings by a different access road (Gk. *met' hodos*), it is nevertheless the same complex that one tries systematically to think through. That is why dogmatic systems that show large differences in method may still be marked by deep kinship in content. The beginning student is therefore advised not to let himself be deterred by the divergences in definition, to say nothing of an obligation to choose between them. Pivotal, in any case, is the systematic and thorough reflection on the salvation given in Christ.

2.5 SYSTEMATIC AND THOROUGH REFLECTION ON SALVATION

One can think his way through salvation in a variety of ways (without ever having exhausted the subject). Every attentive Bible reader does it in his own way. The pastor, in the process of preparing his sermon, does it in a somewhat different way. Again, the person who takes time out to meditate has a method of his own. One can reflect on salvation in order to compose a song about it or to write a conference paper on it;

one can do it to nourish one's own faith or to help others pastorally.

Dogmatic reflection differs from other forms of "thinking-through" by its systematic character. "Systematic" is an adjective derived from a Greek verb that literally means "to set up together," to line up in a row in a correct order. To be able to do that one must first analyze a given object of thought — split it up in a number of different components — in order then to combine those elements in such a way as to make visible both their unique qualities and their interconnections. This double operation of separating and combining, of analysis and synthesis, is a typically intellectual activity. It underlies everything we call science. The concern of science is the intellectual examination and illumination of all of reality known to us. That scrutiny and clarification varies, of course, for every field of inquiry and every object. Methods are often very divergent. But in any case there is this intellectual act of separating things and putting them together. That is the aim of dogmatics: to attain intellectual clarity by ordering the given materials systematically.

Or is this precisely the wrong thing to do when it concerns God and his salvation? After all, we cannot gain intellectual mastery over the salvation of God, can we? It is entirely understandable that many believers have a nervous fear of dogmatics because such activity hinders their personal association with God as a result of the objectivizing distance that must then arise between God and them. Indeed, God on the dissecting-table is no longer God! But there are a good many things in the world that cannot be laid on a cutting-table that can nevertheless still be examined systematically. The love of God demands our personal surrender. But in making that surrender we must have clearly before our minds what that love really is and seeks. To love and to examine are not mutually exclusive activities. (This is also true in the case of earthly love and friendship.) True, if scrutiny is made the final goal it will kill its own object. But if it arises out of love and aims to serve the deepening of that love it can mean a very desirable clarification of the relationship. True love, after all, is the very opposite of being blind. Such great dogmaticians as Augustine, Thomas, Calvin, and Barth have demonstrated how objectification can be the servant of communication and, in fact, be an element in it. It is God's will that we shall also love him with the mind. Sad to say, there are also many systematic theologies that by their scholasticism and intellectualism constitute a "cure" for love. But, as with every activity of the human mind, dogmatics must be judged by its best and not by its worst representatives.

But there is another danger here: "systematic" is a word referring to "system." Is it the purpose of systematic investigation to map out the salvation of God in a well-rounded system? The genuine dogmatician can never altogether suppress the desire to try. He imagines that by an examination of all the angles, wonder, love, and adoration would also rise to the top. He longs for the moment when he as dogmatician will be permitted to know as now he is known by God. But he also knows that this privilege is not granted us within the bounds of this earthly life. Now we know only in part, but some day we shall see face to face. Classical theology makes the distinction between a *theologia in via* (theology under way) and a *theologia in visione* (theology in vision). But in the here-and-now we do not get further than *theologia viatorum* (wayfarers' theology). The believer as dogmatician is also a person under way. But that implies that he is going somewhere and has a goal in view. The system is eschatological; it lies beyond all his earthly possibilities as a limited and sinful human being. But he works energetically toward it as toward his outer limit and horizon. He does not acquiesce in the possession of disconnected and one-sided fragments of knowledge. He wants to give expression to discovered linkages. He wants to view the unity of God's work as the mirror-reflection of the unity of God himself. He knows he will never do more than clarify in part. He has to live, therefore, with vacuums, break-offs, and inconsistencies. But he also knows that only he who searches for the whole picture will look for and discover new connections. Only he who reaches for the unattainable will get to see more of the attainable.

2.6 THE "USEFULNESS" OF DOGMATICS

Still, what is the use of such systematic examination? Is not the truth revealed to little children? And were not the apostles simple fishermen? These two objections call for comment. The "children" to whom the salvation of God is revealed are not the "dumb" ones, the unthinking ones as distinguished from the wise and understanding ones, but those who know that they do not yet know, the receptive ones who live in wonder. The dogmatician-under-way must be such a child, or else he will become a narrow-minded and conceited pedant. And as for the apostles, were they such simple fishermen? In any case, in fellowship with their Lord they left the simple-fisherman stage a long distance behind them. That is especially clear in the case of Peter. And the thirteenth apostle added to the circle, Paul of Tarsus, became the first theologian of the Christian church.

From the beginning there was in the Christian church an urgent desire to examine the faith intellectually — that is, in the nature of the case, among those who had a special gift for such examination and felt a special calling. And the church both appreciated and stimulated that urge. In a variety of ways the church proved to need dogmatics — for its preaching and catechizing, for its dialogue with non-Christian intellectuals, and for its refutation of erroneous developments in its own midst. The first well-rounded dogmatics, that of Irenaeus (d. 185), was named "Against Heresies." The question of the usefulness of dogmatics has been answered clearly and positively by church history. In the continuing process of the interpretation of the gospel, each time in other vocabularies and idioms and to succeeding generations of people, the thorough examination and clarification of the salvation handed down to us has been an indispensable source of support. This is not to deny that there has also been a great number of sterile and even harmful dogmatic systems. Melanchthon, himself a dogmatician, sighed over "the mad rage of the theologians" (*rabies theologorum*) — since then a standing expression. For it is strange but true that in this discipline, which deals with that which far transcends our understanding, a massive amount of opinionated argument, self-conceit, and aggression has been openly displayed. As a result, church members have often found theology so inhibiting and even horrifying that for many only an "undogmatic" Christianity can be considered the true version.

But precisely then, as if by an argument from absurdity, it

becomes evident how indispensable dogmatic reflection is for the spiritual vitality of the church and its place in the world. For aversion to thorough intellectual reflection is almost always accompanied by an emotional and, therefore, amorphous understanding of the faith, which does not lead to an intelligible, articulated transmission of it. And if this extreme is avoided, then it is often because people bring with them a fair amount of unconsciously held dogmatic information. And that, too, is bad because that which is unconscious is as such not thought through and therefore untested. As a result of all this, aversion to dogmatics in a given church communion is in many instances both a symptom and a cause of the fact that such a church plays no role in the intellectual culture of its environment, simply because its members have not learned to express their faith on an intellectual plane.

It would appear that these days a sense of the importance of dogmatics in broad Christian circles is stronger than it has been for a long while. This state of affairs is bound up with two things: growing secularization and higher levels of education. Many more church members than in the past ask for theological schooling of some kind. In the secularized climate in which they live they are challenged from without and from within to account for what they believe. Theological books that speak to this need sell in numbers of copies that were inconceivable in the past.

It would seem, then, that the usefulness of dogmatics has been established. In the heading of this section the word occurs between quotation marks, however. This is not only because it is such a stale eighteenth-century word but also because we must not link this notion of utility (nowadays we would speak of "relevance") too closely with the study of dogma. For dogmatics is really done well only by people who undertake this study not for the sake of any utility they see in it but because they cannot help themselves. This is true, for that matter, of any science. It is studied simply because a person wants to know. And it is precisely then that discoveries are made that prove later to be very useful.

The genuine dogmatician also wants to know. Echoing Anselm he says: "I believe in order that I may understand" (*Credo ut intelligam*). Not that he does dogmatics as a mere hobby; as a believer it is his aim to express his love for God in it. He seeks to love God also, and particularly, with his mind and thus grow in fellowship with him. The proper practice of dogmatic study is part of the sanctification of human life. But this is never done in isolation; it is done in the fellowship of faith and in its service and (by way of this fellowship, as a rule) that of the world. Within this context it automatically becomes fruitful and relevant. It represents *one* charisma in the body of Christ in the midst of many others. A church composed of only dogmaticians would no longer be a church but a research center. "Are all dogmaticians?" Paul might have added to his list in 1 Corinthians 12:29-30. The proportion of dogmatic specialists in the fellowship needs only to be small. But those who can benefit from their work need to be many.

2.7 THE TWO WORLDS OF DOGMATIC STUDY

The dogmatician lives in two worlds, that of faith and that of scholarship. Occasionally, nettlesome questions are raised about this duality, especially by outsiders. People then usually overlook the fact that every student in every branch of learning lives in two worlds. On the one hand, he is most intimately involved with a piece of reality that he shares with others: the doctor with human corporeality, the astronomer with the world of stars, the zoologist with animal life, the legal scholar with the laws of the land, the sociologist with a part of life in society, the literary historian with a slice of literary history, and so forth. As a rule, the urge to make a more thorough study of a given area of reality arises only when a person is humanly seized by a fascination with it. Then he begins "to approach" that field of experience "scientifically" — as it is put. This is a striking way of putting it because it indicates that a person first takes some distance from the field of study, the distance of dispassionate observation, which a person then tries to bridge by a process of reflection. So the scholar lives between experience and reflection.

This is also true of the dogmatician. He lives in his own faith-communion in which the material by which he is nurtured is mediated to him from the sources of revelation. But at the same time he takes his place at some distance from that faith-communion so that he might see it in sharper focus and define what exactly is happening there. And on account of the distance between the sources and the present, he will look not only to take note of what he sees but to look critically: What precisely is the salvation that is being transmitted here? And is it being transmitted well?

So the dogmatician oscillates between experience and reflection. Without the dissociation of reflection he cannot do his work well in terms of *method*. Without participation in the experience of Bible and church he cannot do his work well in terms of *content*. Such oscillation is not without dangers. C. S. Lewis once wrote that there are theologians in the bottom of hell who are more interested in their own thoughts about God than in God himself. For that reason it is important that a dogmatician should also preach regularly. He will then create a counterweight to his intellectual preoccupations. But he cannot escape the two worlds. Knowing the dangers and taking the risks, however, he can live with the tensions.

In the next two chapters we shall, therefore, have to look at dogmatics from two angles: first, from the angle of the field of experience on which it is focused — Bible, church, and faith; second, from the angle of the world of scholarship in which it occupies a place of its own — the study of religions, Bible exegesis, church history, and the like. The two distinct contexts will illuminate the dogmatic enterprise from two directions. The more connections we see, the clearer its own field of study and method will become to us.

Three

CONTEXTS WITHIN THE PERSPECTIVE OF FAITH

3.1 THE BIBLE

The dogmatician, like every other believer, must first be nourished by the experiences on which he is professionally and intellectually focused. A person who does not love nature must not specialize in botany. A person who is a-musical is well advised not to choose the history of music as his field of study. For the believing Christian, of whatever church or creed, the Bible will — perhaps not in a psychological-chronological sense but certainly logically — be the foremost source of nourishment. That is where it started: there one finds the center, Jesus Christ; there one can hear the speech of the primary witnesses concerning the Way on which we have to travel. The dogmatician must first of all be able to read the Bible, as it is done everywhere in Christian churches, as basically *one* message from God, and as a summons to each of us to faith and obedience. If he should be able to approach the Bible only scientifically he would not even be able to do that one thing well. For this specialized approach is dependent on prior experience. He must also be able to meditate on a Bible passage personally; he must be able, as an ordinary church member, to take part in a church service; and if he is qualified and has the opportunity, he should also, if at all possible (as we remarked earlier), preach regularly in order to nurture others with the Word of Scripture.

This is sometimes called the "naive" use of the Bible. That description may be well intentioned but it may easily cause us to forget that precisely this use is direct, personal, and existential, and that here the roles, as compared with a scientific approach, are reversed: I do not approach the Bible critically but I see how God, by way of the biblical witness, approaches me critically. By comparison the intellectual approach may easily be a shallow form of reading the Bible and even an avoidance of encounter. There is a very real danger that the dogmatician immerses himself in Christology and pneumatology, for example, in order not to be confronted with Jesus Christ and the Holy Spirit.

We also have to point out, however, that next to this necessary and fruitfully "naive" orientation is the possibility of a so-called "undogmatic" orientation to Scripture, which, so far from inspiring and directing the dogmatic enterprise, frustrates it. All kinds of churches, groups, and sects call themselves "true to Scripture" and at their theological training schools they only want "to adhere to the Bible." Upon closer scrutiny, however, it turns out that for these scholars the Bible contains no surprises. On every page they search for, and find, a certain set of fundamental truths (hence the name "Fundamentalism"). Texts that have a bearing on these truths are even printed in bold letters in their Bible editions. Clearly there is present here a most detailed set of pointers that precedes the act of reading Scripture. This existing hermeneutic and dogmatics tends not to be open to criticism. The waters of the spring do not flow anymore; they are now stored up in buckets. This form of fidelity to the Bible makes dogmatics impossible. For "every scribe who has been trained for the kingdom of heaven is like a householder who brings out of his treasure what is new and what is old" (Matt. 13:52). That process is possible only if the "naive" association with the Bible remains really naive, that is, full of wonder and of eagerness for new discoveries. As a rule the dogmatic enterprise flourishes only in those churches where no limits are placed upon the sense of wonder. The defense of the authority of Scripture by itself does not mean that the defenders are open to what the Bible has to say.

But where that openness is present and a naive sense of wonder accompanies our reading of Scripture, we irrevocably run into problems our intellects cannot ignore. The Bible is a library, full of divergent and sometimes, to our minds, even contradictory viewpoints. People who take its authority to be a kind of law that requires that we read the Bible as a book of precise and internally coherent information can no longer claim they are reading the text for what it really says, and are bound to mess up exegetically. The authority of the Bible is not the authority of a code but that of a road. For it describes the way God pointed to and went with his people — before Christ, in Christ, and in the earliest churches. Not everything on that journey by far has the same authority for us. Take another image, of a center, which has fields immediately adjacent to it, and a distant periphery. What in Scripture belongs to one and what to the other? Needed here is the guidance of the Spirit in the believing community to lead it in all truth. This takes us to the next section.

3.2 CHURCH AND CONFESSION

The mistaken fidelity to the Bible we just described as being deadly to dogmatics is rooted also in the attempt to read the Bible apart from the great process of transmission that has gone on now, in churches and in the creeds, for nearly twenty centuries. We call it "tradition." This is another context of experienced reality from which the dogmatician cannot and may not withdraw himself. We are all situated somewhere in church history and we all concretely slake our thirst from broad or narrow streams, from ancient or recent currents. (This is also true of the "fundamental" ones, but they prefer not to think of it for fear of relativism.) From Christ and from the biblical witnesses have issued an enormous history of effects (*Wirkungsgeschichte*). In that history the work of the Holy Spirit has taken shape and still takes shape. In the farewell discourses recorded in John one reads these mysterious words:

> I have yet many things to say to you, but you cannot bear them now. When the Spirit of truth comes, he will guide you into all the truth; for he will not speak on his own authority, but whatever he hears he will speak, and he will declare to you the things that are to come. He will glorify me, for he will take what is mine and declare it to you. (John 16:12-14)

We are here broaching the difficult problem of Scripture and tradition. It is clear that the Christ to be preached is the norm by which all the developments and deviations of the transmission process have to be judged. But, conversely, it is also true that the Spirit is the norm of the full truth concerning Christ. The believer, hence also the dogmatician, has no choice but to station himself somewhere within that transmission process. As a rule, that is a position assigned to him by birth and education. That is why the church, next to the Bible, plays a controlling role amid the experiences by which the dogmatician is nurtured and on which he reflects. The Eastern Orthodox, Roman Catholic, and Anglican or Episcopal churches especially put great stress on this rootage in tradition, so much so that the Bible as component in the transmission process sometimes threatens to lose its inspiring and critical significance over against that process. The Protestant churches, which run exactly the opposite danger, try to escape both dangers by concentrating the nurturing authority of the church in certain specific creeds — also called "the confession" in the singular — which are generally intended as a roadmap showing how the Bible is to be read in a given church-communion. This does not solve the problem, however. To speak of "Scripture and Confession" as the basis of preaching, faith, and also dogmatics may have a liberating as well as a shackling effect upon dogmatics. If the idea is that our understanding of the faith has no authority in itself but spurs us on to a way of listening to the Scriptures that transcends the confession, then the dogmatician knows himself called to freedom within the tradition of his confession and entitled, if necessary, to contradict his own confession from within the Bible. Regrettably, however, the term "confessional dogmatics" is generally understood to mean the opposite: the dogmatician may not, on the basis of wider or other experiences and insights, exceed certain churchly limits. His task is then viewed especially as that of confirming and justifying tradition. It is for this reason that such a programmatic-confessional theology hardly plays a role in the "great" dogmatic tradition. Like the biblicistic theology mentioned earlier, this confessional theology functions in a climate in which there is no room for exploration beyond the usual bounds.

On this score a shift has clearly taken place, not in the least in the Netherlands. In earlier times the dogmatician, in particular the professor of dogmatics at the seminary or university, was more or less viewed as the authoritative ideologist of his church, the transmitter of the traditional and official articulation of the faith. That image still haunts many people. However, to the extent that the churches are increasingly challenged by secularization, the ecumenical movement (see 3.3), and an array of new questions, and so become more pluralistic themselves, dogmaticians are expected to play not the role of church-ideologists but that of pioneers and pathfinders. They are at liberty, if they think it necessary, to criticize their own tradition. By that token they are granted the freedom without which no science can flourish. The risks of individualism or even of cacophony do not outweigh this advantage.

But dogmatics cannot operate without the confessional dimension, without a root-system in the living church with its tradition. When the dogmatician places himself above the confessions, he places himself outside the reality in terms of which, and on which, it is his calling to reflect. He must gratefully think through and give expression to the soundings-indepth and the related decisions of his church or confession. But they have no final authority. Scripture is above them and may, through the medium of dogmatic reflection, complement, criticize, and relativize the confessional tradition.

3.3 THE ECUMENICAL DIMENSION

The word of Scripture can illumine our journey like a flash of lightning and lead us away from the path of tradition. Luther's experience is a classical example of this. Still, as a rule this is not what happens with transconfessional discoveries in dogmatics. The Bible illumines the tradition but tradition also illumines the Bible. Christ and the Spirit are both norms but in a relation of reciprocity—albeit a reciprocity that cannot be reduced to a neat formula. But every believer at times makes the discovery that, more or less apart from the familiar tradition he trusted, he gained new insight in redemption in Christ. Very often this insight came via the channels of other traditions. For the believer this may be an experience; for the dogmatician it is a mandate: in order to grow in insight in salvation and to let his own confessional tradition share in this growth he will have to take note of what the Spirit has given us by way of other transmission processes. In other words, he must live and think not only confessionally but also ecumenically. This presupposes the conviction, of course, that the Spirit has not restricted his operation to the particular tradition of the dogmatician. The person who is afraid to assume this position, at least as a working hypothesis, is bound to fall short as a practitioner of real dogmatics and remains stuck in dogmatics as a group ideology.

Since today the sphere of ecumenicity seems so self-evidently one, if not *the*, domain of experience in which the dogmatician must make himself at home, it may be well especially to point out its limits. As a rule a person is rooted in a church or a specific confession, not in the worldwide church (whatever that may be). Perhaps a few top functionaries in Geneva constitute an exception to that rule. But among the ones I know or have known that is not the case. On the contrary, they are the ones who say that in order to extend themselves ecumenically to an advanced degree they feel a strong need to secure their own confessional base. The domain of ecumenicity is not a domain of experience in the way that the Bible and tradition are; it is rather a consciously pursued process of exploration, osmosis, and exchange. And even then one has to make a strict choice; there is simply no real possibility of appropriating everything. One would only sink in a boundless morass of normlessness.

But if our circle of experience looks out upon a horizon narrower than the world of ecumenicity, we as theologians fail to do justice to the gospel we are called to serve. In our age the prayer that we "may have power to comprehend with all the saints what is the breadth and length and height and depth"

(Eph. 3:18) can be understood and prayed only ecumenically. A dogmatician who finds his terminus in his own tradition falls short, both as believer and as scholar, of what the Spirit says to the churches. The least that can be asked of a dogmatician is that he immerse himself with a passion in *one* other tradition — even if he should re-emerge with the conviction that his own tradition is more legitimate or richer. That other tradition should not be too close to his own (as when a Reformed person should choose the Christian Reformed Church tradition, or a Roman Catholic the old Catholic); on the other hand, it should be within "hearing" distance. In our pluralistic world one should not as a rule have to travel far. Cooperation on a local level between, for example, the Catholic parish and the Reformed church often brings with it optimal opportunity. But other encounters, as for instance with Episcopal and Methodist churches, are also important. There must always be a few dogmaticians who can interpret and assimilate ecclesiastical and theological life on the European continent.* By contrast, it seems to me that for Protestants the road to a vital relationship with Eastern Orthodox churches is probably too long, the odd specialist excepted.

Much has already changed. In the past we did not read theological works rooted in other traditions. Today, at least in the Netherlands, Protestant and Roman Catholic professors of dogmatics substitute for each other in lecture rooms. For this process of maturation, certain language skills are indispensable. The dogmatician must really be able to speak two modern languages and at least read a third. That is more than pretheological students are generally given. But it is the price to be paid for the ecumenical dimension of the discipline.

One must expect the ecumenical dimension to exert a relativizing influence on the confessional. One learns that in other traditions certain elements of the faith have been developed to a much greater extent than in one's own (for example, the tradition of prayer, the emotional assimilation of salvation, the ascetic and ethical aspects, the way the Lord's Supper is under-

---

*The author, speaking from his situation in the Netherlands, here recommends acquaintance with church life in the "Anglo-Saxon world." I have substituted "the European continent." — Trans.

stood and experienced, the stress on conversion or sanctification of life, etc.). One notices how in other traditions the tensions associated with the transcendence and immanence of God, election and responsibility, Scripture and tradition, institution and fellowship, justification and sanctification, and so forth, are experienced and resolved — or endured — very differently from among ourselves. Still, the Spirit proves to be working there also. That knowledge can create dogmatic confusion and uncertainty, but a dogmatician must take that risk. Only then can he be serviceable to the process by which churches grow together under one Lord and by one Spirit. What could not and did not have to happen in ages past is now, both in terms of the dogmatician's faith and his scholarship, a "must" for him.

3.4 PERSONAL FAITH AND EXPERIENCE

All that is said in the Bible and experienced in the church, confessionally and interconfessionally, envisions one goal: that people will come to personal faith, acceptance, trust, and obedience. We deliberately chose the word "personal," not "individual." The individual (lit., that which cannot be divided any further; Gk. *atomos*) is a person considered in abstraction from the world around him. Such a being can in fact only be *thought*. A human being is not an individual, however, but a person, a being existing in relation to an entire world and especially to other persons, in an unremitting process of receiving and giving. We can therefore speak of personal faith as the final goal of the gospel without at the same time lapsing into individualism. Personal faith participates in a suprapersonal history of redemption. But we would fail to do justice to the role of the Bible, the church, and the ecumenical dimension in the work of the dogmatician if we did not at this point speak of his personal faith.

Dogmaticians do not as a rule like to speak about their personal faith. They do not think it is relevant unless they can give expression to it in dogmatic and hence in general categories. They easily fall under suspicion in certain devout circles, therefore, of having a detached and emaciated faith and hence cannot be counted among the "converted": "The point is not whether you are a master in divinity but whether you are mastered by

Divinity." And, indeed, the dogmatician is constantly threatened by the danger that his objectivizing activity will choke off the living encounter (see under 2.5). But then objectivizing reflection has been cut off from its root and has become a game in which it chokes to death. Such derailments are quickly forgotten, however. The dogmatics that braves the test of time is always a testimony to the faith that seeks understanding. Faith, says Karl Barth somewhere, "is the *conditio sine qua non* of theological science."

The problem begins to take on another aspect when this personal faith appears to remove itself, or actually does remove itself, from the soil of the biblical and churchly tradition. Such a shift is very well possible because the believer draws not only from these wellsprings but also from an entire network of different experiences: nurture and training, economic circumstances, one's personal ups and downs, cultural influences, political conflicts, and so forth. These experiences not only do not leave the focus of faith unaffected but tend very often to bring with them a new slant on the gospel. In changed situations people begin to read the Bible with new eyes: new words and patterns of thought begin to light up while the old lose their forcefulness. The dogmatician undergoing such experiences may then get the feeling that he is losing touch with his tradition and confession. His own personal faith begins to be out of step with that of his associates. He is in danger of becoming a lonely figure or a rebel.

Sometimes this situation is the result of the individualism that threatens so many practicing theologians (as it does, for that matter, scholars in the humanities): I mean the drive to prove one's competence with new finds and brilliant "discoveries." Much of this disappears as fast as it came up because these finds fail to bring to light, or into a fresh perspective, any essential elements of the biblical message. Applicable here is a wise saying stemming, I believe, from professor Isaac van Dijk (c. 1900): "To say something that has never been said before you is to run the risk of saying something that will never be said again after you either."

But the situation may also be quite different. Some theologians have a special gift for sensing the shifts taking place in a given culture and in the human mind; they are people who experience existence very differently from previous generations, and from their new vantage point they put new questions to the Bible and tradition, questions to which they clearly receive surprising new answers. We may call to mind examples like Augustine, Luther, Wesley, or, more recently, Barth's commentary on Romans (2d ed., 1922), Bonhoeffer's *Letters and Papers from Prison*, Moltmann's *Theology of Hope* (1964), Küng's *The Church* (1967). In every one of these instances personal faith presents itself in a new form and language as a result of a shift in the understanding of life. This may be the cause of large-scale conflicts; many view it as proof of a fatal estrangement from Scripture and tradition; many others, especially among the younger ones, welcome it as that interpretation of the gospel which brings home to them anew — or at last — its truth and relevancy.

Naturally, neither reaction is by itself proof of the (il)legitimacy of the new position. The "innovator" will have to be prepared to pay the price for his discovery by listening intently to the resulting criticism, by renewed Bible reading, by evaluating the counterelements in the tradition, by remaining in dialogue, and by engaging in self-examination. The more ready he is to pay this price, the more likely the chance that he will be accepted as genuine and integrated into the community of faith. In time it will be clear that the person who had the courage to stand alone did not remain alone.

In earlier times such a solitary "prophet" would almost always automatically be regarded a "heretic." We have become more cautious with the use of that epithet. Many church teachers started out as heretics. That is true even of Thomas Aquinas. Conversely, heresy often was the name given to the insight that suffered defeat in a given conflict. The appearance of heresy is easily created when someone posits as central the unresolved and ignored problems that threaten the established doctrinal position. In the present pluralistic age the word *heretic* has become less a pejorative epithet than a name of honor. We would almost forget, then, that someone may be so driven by a series of experiences that his personal faith and theology affect the very nerve of the tradition of faith. The question is, who then is authorized to establish this fact and to correct the erring one? Of pontificating pronouncements from popes, bishops, and synods, we have had enough. Still, sometimes the fog has to be cleared up. This, then, must preferably be prepared by an open, nonthreatening exchange of ideas in a theological circle over a long period of time. Not that this will always yield a "final judgment." If there is a penultimate judgment it is that of church history, in which faith perspectives either become fruitful or disappear in time. But that "time" may cover a span of centuries.

In the last few decades we have seen still other examples of estrangement and/or ahead-of-the-pack thinking: the unheard-of phenomenon of groups of believers, previously not at all part of the dogmatic process, who began to intervene in it. Pacesetting dogmaticians, it turned out, had been giving expression to the faith in a way that was hardly recognizable to those who had learned to read the Bible from the perspective of a very different set of experiences. We have in mind especially the blacks in Africa and the United States, the exploited in Latin America, the women in the First World. In terms of their points of view new forms of doing theology arose: black theology, liberation theology, feminist theology. In their best works they give evidence of new discoveries made in Scripture. To the "official" practitioners of dogmatics they pose the question of what unconscious conditioning factors have had their distorting or inspiring effect on them. It is hardly disputable that a well-paid Western European professor in theology sitting behind his desk will read the gospel differently from the neo-Baptist in a concentration camp in Siberia or an illegal union leader languishing in a Chilean prison. It is evidently not enough to refer to the Bible, the creedal tradition, and the transconfessional dimensions of ecumenicity as the funding sources of dogmatics. Even when we have these in common, opposite experiences may make our interpretations of the gospel mutually unintelligible. Or is it our duty radically to exclude the factor of our life experiences because revelation is something totally different from experience? But who can jump over his own shadow? Is it our calling perhaps to work toward a new kind of ecumenicity, one that serves to integrate all the points-of-entry suggested by experience? But where are the minds and hearts that can embrace all this? Can we even take over the verbalizations of the other? Or must it be our goal to seek a new concentration and by this route achieve a new diversity — by viewing dogmatics as critical reflection on the praxis of human existence in action and suffering (*actio et passio*)? (See Gustavo Gutiérrez, *A Theology of Liberation* [Orbis, 1973].) Must ethics and experience be the primary sources of funding the dogmatic enterprise instead of the Bible and the church? Or is that a false set of opposites? Here lie *the* big dogmatic questions of the near future. We shall return to them at a later stage (5.4).

Four

CONTEXTS IN THE SCIENTIFIC DOMAIN

4.1 IS DOGMATICS A SCIENCE?

In 2.7 we discussed the two worlds, that of experience and that of scientific reflection, in which every systematic thinker, including the dogmatician, must play his role. At that time we briefly referred to the tensions associated with that situation. The dogmatician has to hold at arm's length that in which he participates and from which he lives. As a thinker he has to take some distance from himself. His intellect puts itself at some remove from existence. We have seen (2.5) that this assumption of distance is not impossible, provided *participation* is the framework within which and for the sake of which the assumption of distance takes place.

But this is only one of the two fronts on which the dogmatician has to defend his work. He has to justify his reflection before the bar of existence, but he also stands before the bar of science. Over and over the question flares up whether dogmatics can claim to be a *bona fide* science. It is then asserted that its work both possesses and misses certain characteristics that keep it from falling under the definition of science (*Wissenschaft*).

For centuries this standpoint was also taken in the Christian church. Augustine, following Plato, made a sharp distinction in his *De Trinitate* (XII–XIV) between the sciences (*scientiae*) and wisdom (*sapientia*). The first he saw as focused on the exploration of this world. Theology, however, is a form of *sapientia* because it is focused on the love of God as the highest good toward which we must strive. Theological reflection arises from this endeavor and must serve it. (Today we would call this the orientation to praxis.) Earthly sciences by themselves do not serve this goal, though they may point and even lead to it.

This view of dogmatics remained dominant till some time in the thirteenth century, when Plato's authority was pushed back in favor of Aristotle's. Aristotle saw science and wisdom as a unity, in which wisdom has to be considered the highest science. The same century saw the rise of the universities with their departments of theology. At the universities the orientation was strongly Aristotelian. Thomas Aquinas, who developed his dogmatics on the basis of Aristotelianism, posited at the beginning of his *Summa Theologica* that dogmatics is a science (I.1.2). According to Aristotle the true science is mathematics, and just as it derives its theorems from axioms, so according to Aquinas theology deduces its doctrinal positions from revealed principles. But Duns Scotus and later Thomists believed that these principles lacked the self-evident quality of mathematical axioms. Augustine's notion of the practical origin and aim of theology again gained ground.

In Reformation theology there was a strong tendency to view dogmatics not as a science but as *sapientia*. An interesting exception was that offered in the classic dogmatic textbook *Synopsis purioris theologiae* (1625), the so-called Leiden Synopsis, which defined dogmatics as "the science or wisdom concerning divine matters" and claimed for it the name of science because faith entails knowledge that relates to preceding or inferred principles (*Disputatio* I:15ff.).

That debate never ended. Under Kantian influence it gained new impetus because Kant sought to tie the concept of science to the spatial-temporal reality of experience and viewed faith as a conclusion ("postulate") of the moral consciousness. He himself regarded the second as the higher form of knowledge. But in the then-emerging secularized intellectual climate of Europe and North America (which has since remained), his sharp separation of pure and practical reason, of the theoretical and the active, has been especially influential. So it would seem that Augustine's view won out. But whereas for him and his followers wisdom was higher than science, now dogmatics was viewed rather on a lower level because it could not base itself on commonly recognized experience, but could only systematize the "subjective" feelings and convictions of a specific community of faith. In the nineteenth century the issue became a matter of great practical significance because the question was whether dogmatics properly belonged at the many newly founded universities or whether it could better be taught at a church-related theological school or seminary.

The answer to the questions referred to clearly depends on one's definition of "science." If we define science as a methodical conceptual elaboration of certain data of experience, then by that definition dogmatics is a science. But if we regard the data that lend themselves to such elaboration as being restricted, say, to the fields of the natural sciences, and take the "conceptual" to be the organization of individual phenomena under general laws, then dogmatics is not a science; but the same applies to history and most other humanities. One is therefore well-advised not to construe the domain of scientific research too narrowly by a preconceived restrictive definition of what constitutes science. The world of experience consists of many fields and layers which themselves offer to the person investigating them a variety of very different methods suited to the purpose of conceptual exposition.

This would seem to be an argument to permit too many rather than too few disciplines and methodologies in the modern view of the university. But even then dogmatics is unique in the sense that its field of experience (the faith of the biblical witnesses and the church community) does not seem able to claim general validity. That is certainly the case in those instances where dogmatics functions as the legitimizing ideology of a certain church community. But now that ecumenical dialogue in dogmatics has been stepped up to such a high degree (and methods so strongly converge), the field of experience on which dogmatics is focused has become so broad both in time and in space that it can hardly still be viewed, in the midst of the sciences, as a private domain. And this the less to the degree that we become aware of how intensely bound to time and place what we call *the* domain of science really is. Our university notion of science, which dates from after the Enlightenment, was formed and advanced by prospering white men in the service of the needs and interests of a society characterized by industry and technology. The concept of science, so variable in differing ages and parts of the world, also fluctuates along with the "spirit" of a given period. In that light one can say it is likely that in the near future there will be a greater rather than a lesser need for dogmatics at the universities, considering our pluralistic culture; for example, departments of Jewish and Islamic studies.

The question whether dogmatics is entitled to a recognized place in the university setting is of great importance for a university itself, because the answer is an indication of the notion of science that prevails there — in the first place, for the admissibility to the discussion of the question concerning God. For the study of dogmatics itself the question whether it occurs within or outside the university framework is of much less importance. In principle, it needs only the framework of the theological disciplines (see the following subdivisions of chap. 4). It can therefore be adequately situated in a seminary or a theological school.

In practice the issue has been resolved in very different ways. In Germany, Switzerland, Denmark, and other countries, dogmatics (both Protestant and Catholic) is "simply" taught at the universities. This is also the case in Scotland; in England the study of dogmatics has been entrusted to church "colleges" that often enjoy close ties with the universities. In the United States, which officially maintains a sharp separation between church and state, lectures in dogmatics are offered at denominationally sponsored seminaries, many of which are also located very near university campuses. After World War II many universities were augmented with a religion department and also make considerable use of what the seminaries have to offer to students who wish to immerse themselves in the basic questions of religion.

In the Netherlands one may find as the *Sitz im Leben* for academic instruction in dogmatics four different systems: church-sponsored graduate schools in theology, special universities (the Free University in Amsterdam and the Catholic University at

Nijmegen), special privileges at certain state universities (the so-called *duplex ordo*), and a number of seminaries located near universities. For the content, method, or level of this instruction these various arrangements make little or no difference.

By way of conclusion we must for a moment return to the beginning. There has been a centuries-long debate on the question of whether dogmatics is science or sapience. The second concept, which is hardly in use anymore, still continues to be relevant; this is because dogmatics differs from many other disciplines in that it is not descriptive but attains its goal only in personal decisions with regard to the ultimate questions of truth. It takes more than "science" to make one's own choices—and to justify those choices—with the help of Augustine, Thomas, Calvin, Barth, and Rahner. One may call that extra dimension "wisdom" or "art" or "creative synthesis" or something else. But it is precisely this extra dimension that constitutes the essence of dogmatics. Otherwise one remains stuck in biblical theology and/or the history of dogma and theology. The repetition of confessional standpoints is not dogmatics either—unless it is the fruit of one's own independent study and insight. This element of sapience is not in conflict with the science element; rather, with Aristotle we would say that it is the top of it. It is indispensable also in a variety of other so-called "normative" sciences. That is, it is the seasoning in the soup of a truly intellectual culture.

4.2 DOGMATICS AND BIBLE SCHOLARSHIP

In 3.1 we noted how openness-in-faith to the testimony of Scripture is the prime wellspring of experience from which the dogmatician must draw his material. He draws from it, first of all, in the immediate, say, "naive" manner in which this is done in Christian churches throughout the world. But as dogmatician he is expected to be able to read the Bible in still another way: not only believingly but also scientifically. In making that statement we are broaching a problem that calls forth enormous tensions for the contemporary dogmatician.

For centuries this was not the case. The dogmatician was deemed to have no second way of reading the Scripture in addition to the "naive." It was his task only to order systematically the material that came to him by this route. But as we remarked in 3.1, the "naive" reading of the Bible is frequently not in the least naive, and this was even more true of the dogmatician. He oriented himself, or had to orient himself, to the guideposts existing in his church, the *regula fidei* in the form of liturgical or cathechetical creeds, dogmatic declarations, conciliar decrees, or church confessions. He was expected to read and interpret Scripture in their light. In addition, often there were still other directions for reading Scripture, less binding but more generally in use, like the allegorical method for explaining the Old Testament so as to harmonize it with the New.

In the sixteenth century it was Humanism on the one hand and the Reformation on the other that began focusing on the study of the Bible by itself, apart from the traditional ecclesiastical framework. A concern arose to go back to the sources (*ad fontes*); the original languages were studied, and an attempt was made to find the literal, and not so much the allegorical, sense. Statements in Scripture, though inspired by the Spirit, also had to be read in terms of the author's intent (*ē mente auctoris*), and obscure texts needed to be explained in the more immediate or broader context of Bible book or canon (*sacra scriptura sui ipsius interpres*). Perhaps the most impressive monument of this new way of interpreting Scripture is Calvin's series of commentaries, which, because of its undogmatic, sober openness to the words of the text, is still consulted far and wide.

But just as at an earlier time church traditions could act to block an unbiased reading of Scripture, so after 1600 the increasingly rigid doctrine of inspiration served to do the same in Protestant churches. Protestants placed the infallible Bible over against the fallible church. That has had an enormously curtailing effect on the nascent Bible sciences. Because all Bible books were judged to be equally inspired, all texts were thought to be equally important and never at odds with each other. In virtue of this static and harmonizing mode of reading Scripture, dogmatics was able to use the Bible as an arsenal of prooftexts for its propositions. That is how dogmatics treated the Bible in the centuries following the Reformation. There were exceptions, however; not everyone muzzled the Bible to the same degree.

But even the use of Scripture made by a person like H. Bavinck in his *Gereformeerde Dogmatiek* still offers clear evidence of how little the texts were allowed to speak for themselves and how extensively they had to serve merely as prooftexts (*loci probantes, dicta probantia*).

Two hundred years ago there developed, in opposition to the scholastic-orthodox doctrine of inspiration, a method of Bible research that is dominant to this day: the so-called literary-historical or historical-critical method. This method ties in with that of the Reformation, on the one hand, but differs from it, radically, on the other, because it does not proceed from the self-revealing God as subject of Scripture but from the human authors. It reads the Bible fundamentally as an expression of the human spirit or, rather, as a library of many such human and therefore historically dated expressions. In the process the multiplicity of the biblical witness came into the light of day and its unity was no longer a premise but at best a conclusion. This method led materially to a radical reconstruction of the course of the biblical histories. For example, the creation story of Genesis 1 and the laws of the Torah were dated in the exile, and several so-called apostolic letters were read as products of later generations.

It is understandable that such Bible scholarship is regarded in nearly all churches, and almost to this very day, with suspicion and resistance; after all, its starting points seem to contradict squarely those of the naive believer's reading of Scripture. Less understandable is the fact that, until recently, dogmatics itself showed little or no interest in the method and results of Bible scholarship — and that while dogmatics and Bible research were done side by side at universities and theological schools. Evidently the new Bible studies had a threatening effect on the age-old department of dogmatics or were at best viewed as immaterial or nonintegrable. Behind that is something to which we have referred earlier: the estrangement that occurs when the scholar has to dissociate himself, thinkingly, from his funding source in experience. The dogmatician had to feel this acutely in his confrontation with Bible scholarship. Can he as a believer read the testament of the Father with the eyes of a notary's clerk? So it happened that dogmatics continued, until well into the twentieth century, to use the Bible in a way that Bible scholars viewed as obsolete or at least as inadequate.

In the forties a shift began to make itself felt. In his extended exposition of Genesis 1 and 2 (*Church Dogmatics* III/1), Karl Barth took leave of the traditional dogmatic manner of reading Scripture but at the same time expressed his regret, in the preface of this and of the following volume, that he received no help from colleagues in Old and New Testament studies and therefore had to develop his own method of reading and exposition. This method, which leaned heavily on the use of concordances and operated within a redemptive-historical perspective, has found few followers in the biblical disciplines, however. But just as Barth designed a biblical hermeneutic from a position in dogmatics, so Bultmann, in the same period, developed one from a position in the arena of Bible scholarship, aided by the philosophy of Heidegger and with the intent to let the Bible speak anew to contemporary people. His hermeneutic, however, found no favor among most dogmaticians because its roots in existentialism offered no room for many components of the Christian faith.

Still, in the fifties and the sixties, the discipline of hermeneutics (the theory of exegesis), having risen from its ashes, became the common ground on which Bible scholars and dogmaticians began to meet and learned to speak a common language. In particular, two men pioneered in this area: Gerhard von Rad from the side of Bible scholarship, with his *Old Testament Theology* (trans. D. M. G. Stalker [Harper & Row, 1962]), and K. H. Mislcotte, from the side of dogmatics, with his book *When the Gods are Silent* (trans. J. W. Doberstein [Harper & Row, 1967]). Under these influences interest in Bible studies grew, especially among the followers of Barth. In the so-called Amsterdam School (F. H. Breukelman, K. A. Deurloo) the modern structuralist hermeneutic even came to be totally at the service of a Barthian dogmatics.

This development meant that while certain hermeneutic results of Bible scholarship had been integrated in dogmatics, not so the historical-critical method itself. It was not until the seventies that dogmatics began to make the multiplicity and occasional contradictions of the biblical writings fruitful for its own work. Before this could happen scholars first had to discover that a number of awkward exegetical finds eventually proved fruitful for the renewal of dogmatic theology. Biblical scholarship often served as gadfly to sting dogmatics into action. In the future, too, we must be prepared for tensions and conflicts. But for now there are clear signs of such fructifying influence. In the orbit of the German language the *Neues Glaubensbuch* (1973; a joint effort by Protestant and Roman Catholic theologians) is a good example. In the Netherlands, I cite as a specimen my *Christian Faith* (trans. S. Woudstra [Eerdmans, 1979]) and, as the most radical instance of the integration of Bible scholarship, E. Schillebeeckx, *Jesus: An Experiment in Christology* (trans. H. Hoskins [Crossroad, 1979; Random House, 1981]).

This last work brings me to the Catholic construal of the relationship between Bible scholarship and dogmatics. This was established in a decree of the Council of Trent concerning the interpretation of Scripture: ". . . that no one relying on his own judgment shall, in matters of faith and morals pertaining to the edification of Christian doctrine, distorting the Holy Scriptures in accordance with his own conceptions, presume to interpret them contrary to that sense which holy mother Church, to whom it belongs to judge of their true sense and interpretation, has held and holds, or even contrary to the unanimous teaching of the Fathers, even though such interpretations should never at any time be published" (*Fourth Session,* April 1546; trans. H. J. Schroeder, O.P.). It is clear that this decree laid a heavy mortgage on Bible scholarship and made it virtually impossible for dogmatics to exercise a critical function over against the church tradition. It was not until Leo XIII and Pius X and later that Bible studies were given a little more leeway to discuss more modern problems. Many scholars in the field have seized the opportunity and made the most of it, with the result that today Catholic biblical scholarship has completely caught up with that of Protestants and can no longer be distinguished from it either in method or in content. Where necessary, it refers to church pronouncements that sound a different note but leaves it to dogmatics to advance the necessary arguments in defense of them. Catholic dogmatics has greatly enlarged its margin of freedom especially by a reinterpretation of church pronouncements. But the Sacred Congregation for the Doctrine of the Faith follows all that is written with a watchful and distrustful eye. When dogmaticians, appealing to modern Bible research, stray too far from the doctrinal tradition, they get into difficulties, as Küng and Schillebeeckx (after the appearance of his previously mentioned book on Jesus) experienced.

A word must also be said in reference to Jewish Bible scholarship because it has had a fructifying and challenging effect on Christian thought. This has taken place, on the one hand, as a result of the Old Testament studies of Martin Buber, in which he elaborated the contrast between the static gods of the Near East and the migratory God of Israel; on the other hand, by the studies of David Flusser concerning the continuity of Jesus especially with the rabbinical Judaism around him. Both of them, together with other prominent figures, called the attention of dogmaticians to the Jewish dimension of the gospel and helped to inspire the construction of a Christology "from below," from the perspective of the (Jewish) man Jesus.

We have two more things to say concerning the relationship between Bible scholarship and dogmatics. From the preceding it follows that in dogmatics the appeal to Scripture has changed profoundly. Increasingly less use is made of isolated texts. When the biblical testimonies are read in their historical contexts, they add up not to a system so much as to a road or journey. That road or journey, it turns out, can repeatedly change direction and offer varying perspectives. It has continued since the apostolic age. How that continuation should take place, as part of the journey of obedience, cannot be laid down in a few simple lines of prose. Again and again the journey must be surveyed in its totality and then related to the situation of the present. That is more difficult, but also more fruitful, than reliance on prooftexts.

Second, the dogmatician whose ear is open to Bible scholarship nevertheless has to maintain his own responsibility and independence toward it, if for no other reason than that the results of Bible scholarship and, to a lesser extent, its methods are so much in process of change. He cannot allow himself to be guided by the latest finds of individual scholars. He will have to orient himself to the consensus that has developed in the preceding decades. Naturally, this consensus can also be out of date. But this also happens frequently to systematic theologies. Not one of us writes his books for all eternity; it is all "way-farers' theology" (*theologia viatorum*). Whether our building is with gold and silver or with wood and hay is not for us to judge, nor even for the coming generations. This fact may not tempt us, however, to think or to write at random. We constantly labor in responsibility toward the biblical witness but also with the responsibility to draw the lines of that witness toward the present. In meeting the first responsibility, dogmatics can be greatly aided by biblical scholarship; in meeting the second it will recognize that biblical scholarship, in view of its special focus, cannot be so helpful. But biblical scholarship cannot relieve the dogmatician even of the first responsibility. In the performance of his task the dogmatician will have to have an ear open in still other directions.

4.3 DOGMATICS AND CHURCH HISTORY

In 3.2 we noted how the dogmatician as believer is fed and funded, so to speak, also by (a part of) church history. For he is rooted in a community of faith that has made its own way and has its own position in the history of the church. But as a scholar he cannot be satisfied merely with this elementary or naive participation in church history. He must objectivize, and then integrate, that participation in a much broader church-historical context. For his work he is therefore also dependent on specialists in the history of the church. Their contribution, like that of Bible scholars, has an "estranging" effect on the dogmatician, rooted as he is in his own church and doctrinal tradition. He begins to view his own tradition as but one stream in a large river basin. The belief that his church took the position that was historically and doctrinally correct, once a certainty, now becomes a question. That question can end in a new certainty but as a rule it will be considerably more nuanced than the stalwart certainty of the beginning. It will also be more fruitful for him if church-historically his estrangement turns into ecumenical involvement (cf. 3.3) and into a deeper and broader personal appropriation of the faith by contact with other models of it and with great believing personalities (cf. 3.4).

The dogmatician can attempt to escape the relativizing influences of church history by examining everything he finds there "in the light of the Bible." But merely to speak of the Bible in the singular very often implies a simple selection of a few biblical theses handed down by one's own tradition. The application of biblical norms to the history of the church tends then to come out in justification of the position of one's own church, and thus is circular reasoning. If the history of the church is the domain of the Spirit, and if the Spirit blows where it wills, our dogmatic insight can only be fed and structured by the continuing interaction between Scripture and tradition (3.2). And not even so-called heretics are *a priori* excluded from that tradition. The label "heretic" was applied, by both parties in a dispute, to those who fell outside of certain groups. It was often their mission to give expression to parts of the truth that had been neglected or suppressed. The dogmatician has no license to exclude this possibility without consulting the church historians with some concern for detail.

Generally, within the field of church history, the dogmatician is judged to be mainly or exclusively interested in that subdivision which is variously described, depending on regional or ecclesiastical or university traditions, as "the history of dogma," or "the history of theology," or "the history of doctrine," or whatever other terms there may be. In practice this discipline comes down to being research in the history of dogmatic reflection from the postapostolic era to the present. For the dogmatician a thorough knowledge of this field is equally as indispensable as schooling in biblical hermeneutics. (A person wanting to specialize in dogmatics in a postgraduate setting is well-advised, in my opinion, to take Old and New Testament studies as well as the history of theology, in addition to dogmatics, for his doctoral examination.) One cannot fruitfully "dogmatize" if one has not at least first listened to the giants in the history of theology, from Augustine to Barth.

Still, there lurks a danger in this preference. The dogmatician then operates within the bounds of part of the history of ideas and runs the risk of regarding these ideas as free-floating entities. But with ideas that is never and nowhere the case. All ideas have a *Sitz im Leben* in which they arise and to which they are, intentionally or unintentionally, subservient. A person who fails to read the ideas of the great theologians of all times first and foremost as their answers to the questions and challenges of their own time, runs the danger of turning them into colorless abstractions. For that reason the history of theology must always be read in close connection with the history of the church and also in connection with what we call general history.

The difficulty is that we live and believe and theologize within a mammoth network of *Sitz im Leben*: upbringing and reading, personal history, cultural climate, tradition, the prevailing piety in the church, and so on. One's theology can never be understood in terms merely of one or two of these factors. Moreover, much of this material is not retrievable and much of what is retrievable is peripheral to the understanding of it. But it is a good thing that modern church-historiography is open to a variety of these nontheological factors. Nowadays there is special attention for the socioeconomic forces operative in (church) history. These have long been neglected and often cast remarkable light on things. The young Luther and Wesley, for example, cannot be understood apart from them. Still, this too is only one aspect among many and one about which the relevant texts are often silent at that. To fill the vacuum with knowledge drawn from other sources is unscholarly and leads to speculation. In any case, the dogmatician who immerses himself in the history of his discipline needs to be curious concerning the broader context in which his predecessors did their work. He will then understand better why in that work (to his mind) certain elements were overexposed or underdeveloped. And in the process he begins also to understand himself better. He becomes more tolerant toward predecessors and more stringent toward himself.

By way of this detour we may and must return to the history of ideas. For now we need to ask whether and how these ideas can be made fruitful in our present-day context. For that purpose it will often be necessary to slice away another layer of historical material, by refraining at this stage (after first situating the ideas in their original context) from listing all kinds of historical data and noting all kinds of shifts, and by concentrating on the structure of a given world of thought. As an intermediate exercise between history and dogmatics, it may be necessary to engage in the construction of "models" — studies, for example, of the doctrine of God, Christology, and Ecclesiology in certain thinkers as compared with others. We then observe the similarities and the differences in these designs, similarities and differences that make us think. As a result of this process one starts both to relate and to relativize his own work historically. But this is precisely how the dogmatician discovers that, together with all those others, he is still under way on the Way. He will to the best of his abilities do what he saw his predecessors doing; namely, in their time and for their world and cultural stage of development, interpret the vital forces of the gospel that transcends all our human situations and can therefore enter them healingly and with wholesome effect. One Spirit embraces and inspires them all.

4.4 DOGMATICS AND PHILOSOPHY (OF RELIGION)

The third discipline from which dogmatics expects help is philosophy. This assistance is of a fundamentally different sort than that offered by Bible scholarship and church history. Both of these areas concentrate on fields of reality in which dogmatics (not descriptively this time but systematizingly) also has an interest. The interest of philosophy, however, is reality as such, as it presents itself to the reflecting mind. In this context, concepts like revelation, faith, redemptive history, the Holy Spirit, and often God are generally bracketed because they require a different angle of approach than the one with which the philosopher approaches reality. Thus defined, it would seem, then, that dogmatics and philosophy concern themselves with very different matters. But the truth is not that simple. This is evident from the ancient and widespread tradition of instructing pretheological students in the history and fundamentals of philosophy. Those instructions — generally, a year's study — cannot be very deep. Nor is it necessary for a number of theological subdisciplines. That is comforting to students who are hungry for the concrete and do not possess the powers of abstraction without which one cannot independently join the philosophic enterprise.

But for other areas of study some background in philosophy *is* necessary. Among them are the history of theology and dogmatics proper. In 4.3 we noted how essential it is for the dogmatician to have a knowledge of the history of theology. But in that study he is bound to come in contact with the history of philosophy. It is evident that he cannot understand Augustine without some knowledge of Plato, nor Thomas Aquinas and the later (neo-) Thomists without some acquaintance with Aristotle. And in his study of seventeenth-century Protestant scholasticism he also encounters these two philosophers. Protestant theology, from 1800 to the end of the twentieth century, is incomprehensible without Kant and German Idealism. In our century, Bultmann and Tillich cannot be understood apart from Heidegger, nor Miskotte and Noordmans apart from phenomenology, nor Moltmann without Bloch, or Pannenberg without Hegel, or several English theologians without Wittgenstein. This phenomenon is connected with the fact that the dogmatician interprets and systematizes salvation history in the direction of his own time. And the different philosophical schools and fashions offer him substantial help in understanding his own time. They take the temperature of the cultural climate; they are bearers of the present sense of existence and life and often precursors of the one following.

In other words, the dogmatician needs philosophy both to understand his predecessor and to be able to do his own work of interpretation well. He is able to profit from the clarification of life that the philosopher offers him and the conceptual material he presents. From time to time it has happened that difficult dogmatic issues, like that of predestination and free will, or that concerning the objective and the subjective, lost their sharpness in a succeeding period because they could be framed and formulated with the aid of other philosophical concepts. Philosophic thought has influenced that of dogmatics in all kinds of ways: as fructifying or as a temptation, as challenge or enrichment. And we are not even talking about the philosophy of religion. Philosophy has many branches: logic, epistemology, cosmology, anthropology, the theory of science, language philosophy, to name a few. In each of them there is much for the dogmatician to learn that can give breadth and depth to his own thinking, though naturally he cannot take note of everything. He will find that when he incorporates philosophical insights in his dogmatic theory, their content tends to change considerably. That applies to concepts like "spirit," "reason," "life," "freedom," "structure," "history," "existence," and many other such. Within the context of the process of salvation, they lose that absolute or abstract quality they often have in philosophy in order to assume a limited and serviceable role.

Not every theologian has to wade deeply into philosophical questions. But sometime in the course of his training he needs to deal, under one heading or another, with the philosophy of religion. It is very hard, however, to define the contents of that discipline. Is the idea of it that religion must be subjected to philosophical examination? Or that a philosophical view of life is designed on the basis of religious faith? Or is religion here one of the material sources and media for a philosophic construal of reality? Or is its focus the question of how much knowledge and what kind of knowledge human beings can have of God apart from revelation? Do the concerns of the philosophy of religion lie in the "prolegomena," the vestibules of the faith (*praeambula fidei*)? Does it undergird faith with rational arguments, thus being a kind of apologetics? Is philosophy, then, as the old saying has it, "the handmaiden of theology" (*ancilla theologiae*), or is the reverse intended? Or is it a case of two disciplines in dialogue, each speaking from a very different point of view but both talking, at least in part, about the same reality?

I suspect that the Dutch legislators of 1876 had in mind a key discipline in the new state university in which the phenomenon of religion would be studied philosophically and its truth-content established. The philosophy of religion, then, was intended to be a secularized dogmatics. If that was its intent, however, little came of it. Most of its practitioners were and are themselves Christians who deny this pretentious claim. In practice, it generally comes down to a confrontation between a theological and philosophical approach to "the problem of God." That objective, as a rule, offers the scholar(s) more than enough to do.

The first thing that strikes a person is that in Western philosophy, since the time of the Greeks, God functioned especially as a final and inclusive concept serving as capstone of the philosopher's construal of reality. For philosophy, which studies reality in its totality, can only approach God "from below" and know him only insofar as his being can be inferred from that reality or is postulated by that reality. The question, then, is whether this all-embracing end-product of conceptual thought has anything to do with the God of salvation history in Israel, the Father of Jesus Christ, who is often called "the living God" in Scripture. He is not a concept but a person, not an object of thought but an agent who acts. In that context the philosophy-of-religion approach and that of dogmatics have to be mutually exclusive. The first is then the enemy of the second and only needs to be known to be effectively combated. Tertullian (c. 200), appealing to Colossians 2:8, had already cried out: "What has Athens to do with Jerusalem? What the academy with the church?" (*De praescriptione haereticorum* 7.9). Often quoted, too, is the famous *Memorial* of Pascal (1654) titled "Feu," beginning with the words: "God of Abraham, God of Isaac, God of Jacob, not of the philosophers and wise men." The fire-God of revelation is the opposite of the conceptual god of the philosophers (Pascal probably had Descartes in mind). After the Enlightenment this contrast became even sharper, if possible, or was completely changed because many philosophers, moved by their analysis of reality, came to repudiate every God-concept (e.g., Feuerbach, Nietzsche, Sartre, Bloch).

But others—in our century it was particularly Paul Tillich—rejected this contrast between theology and philosophy in its generality. The philosopher who arrives at a certain concept of God must already have observed signals of God in his own experience of reality. Philosophy is often done on the basis of a religious inspiration. The relation between the philosophy of religion and dogmatics can then be captured in a model in which the two are harmonized, as has been the case from Clement of Alexandria (c. 200) via Thomas Aquinas to Paul Tillich; and it continues to be the case today.

At all times there have also been self-consciously Christian philosophers who viewed reality from the perspective of their Christian faith and made an analysis of reality different from their nonbelieving colleagues. For them our world was not closed but open, full of references to a reality that transcends the directly empirical, and apart from which our world cannot be grasped. Among many others I mention the Catholic philosopher Maurice Blondel (1861 – 1949), the Jewish scholar Emmanuel Lévinas (b. 1906), and the Protestant Paul Ricoeur (b. 1913). As a rule they do not make their case on the basis of their own faith, because they believe that their point of view is, in principle, open to all. Their conceptual material is often a great help to the dogmatician in designing the prolegomena of his discipline and sometimes also in construing subdivisions of it, as, for instance, anthropology.

Also, there are certain Christian philosophers who take a big step further and seek to let all their philosophizing be governed and inspired by their faith. In the Netherlands that is the program of "The Philosophy of the Cosmonomic Idea," which is centered at the Free University.* A short distance away from this position is that of the retired philosopher of religion at Utrecht, A. E. Loen, particularly as he presents himself in his book *De Vaste Grond* (1946), where, with the aid of concepts like creation, sin, and redemption, he offers his understanding of reality from a biblical base. But other Christian philosophers believe that with the construction of such a philosophy of revelation one does violence both to philosophy and to revelation. A discussion of this issue falls outside the plan of this book.

It is our purpose, rather, to show how many points of contact there are between dogmatics and (the) philosophy (of religion); and also that these points of contact cannot easily be grasped in one neat definition. But anyone seeking to think through the Christian faith and to put it in conceptual form for his own time has to ask repeatedly how the philosophers, first of all the classic but then also the contemporary ones, looked at the realities of God, man, and the world. One will rarely if ever be able simply to adopt their ideas; but very often, positively or antithetically, they will set him on a certain track. He must be on his guard against letting any one philosopher take him in tow. Rather, let him be an amateur in the good sense of

---

*This philosophy is known in North America from Herman Dooyeweerd's four-volume opus *A New Critique of Theoretical Thought.* — Trans.

the word and, as such, an eclectic. But, to sum up, in the course of his development as a dogmatician, he cannot dispense with some schooling in philosophy, along with his training in Bible scholarship and the history of theology.

4.5 DOGMATICS AND THE HISTORY OF RELIGION

By the history of religion we usually understand the study of non-Christian religions, past and present. Generally considered as falling under this heading are, on the one hand, the so-called primitive religions and those of the Near East as well as of the Mediterranean basin (Egypt, Babylon, Greece, etc.; religions whose influence is noticeable in the Old and the New Testament), and, on the other, the great and still vital religions: Hinduism, Buddhism, Shintoism, Judaism, and Islam. The title "history of religion" is less applicable to this second group. A more spacious category, the "science of religion," is also used. But that is too broad, just as the first is too narrow. So much for the problems of naming the subject.

The importance of this field of study to the theologian is obvious. Our special concern, however, is the question of what it has to say to the dogmatician. Often that seems to be very little. In many departments of theology these two disciplines are at the greatest possible distance from each other and their practitioners tend to have but little mutual contact. This would seem natural where it concerns primitive and some ancient religions. But can it be said that knowledge of living world religions is unimportant to the dogmatician?

In any case, there have repeatedly been times and places where the knowledge of one or more non-Christian religions was a necessity for the dogmatician. Sometimes it was and is appropriate to speak of this as a bitter necessity. We have in mind primarily the time of the church fathers, the centuries beginning with the Apologists and ending with Augustine. During this time Christian thinkers had to make a systematic study of Roman, Hellenistic, and some Oriental religions, and formulate the content of their own faith both offensively and defensively in relation to them. We can say that such a necessity exists wherever the Christian message of salvation has to be interpreted and systematized over against a majority of non-Christians. In India the study of dogmatics bears the stamp of dialogue with modern schools in Hinduism, and in Indonesia dogmatics will give evidence of the daily encounter with Islam. This seems not to be the case in Western Europe or North America, however. But in the heart of the Middle Ages, Thomas Aquinas wrote his *Summa contra Gentiles* (1264) in the face of clearly felt political and intellectual pressure originating in Islam. In later centuries, as a result of the opening up of the world and the work of missions, the need to confront other religions was felt for different reasons. Missiology especially then became the discipline that devoted itself to that confrontation.

For centuries, the non-Christian religions were absent from dogmatic literature, a situation that has only recently begun to change. The mingling of peoples and religions in North America, and the presence in Western Europe of Indian sects and Muslim guest-laborers, serves to bring the dialogue with them and their belief-systems to our very doorsteps. With respect to the Jews, however, this has already been the case for a much longer period. Dogmatics cannot ignore this fact in its work. The World Council of Churches has taken the lead in its "Dialogue with People of Living Faiths and Ideologies," and has succeeded in involving in it a large number of systematic theologians. Toward the end of his life Karl Barth made the statement that if he could do it over he would study the non-Christian religions in particular. Before long no dogmatician will be able to operate without a much more extensive theoretical, and preferably also practical, acquaintance with one or more world religions than his predecessors have had.

In the past there was one part of dogmatics in which "foreign religions" sometimes came briefly into view, namely, in the treatment of "general revelation." But this very name by itself blocked a deeper discussion of these great historic manifestations of revealed religions. As a rule the discussion was restricted to the text of Romans 1:19-23, a discussion in which the second part of the text often virtually cancelled out the first.

Where the dogmaticians failed, historians of religion sometimes tried to fill the vacuum. Their teaching assignment in many instances included "the phenomenology of religion" or "comparative religion" — a field of study that invites reflection on the essential differences between religions. In the Netherlands, G. van der Leeuw and H. Kraemer in particular did not shrink from taking descriptive materials and converting them into systematic statements. But, barring the rare exception, dogmaticians did not follow this lead.

Today, in dogmatics, it will not do simply and briefly to refer to world religions under the heading of "general revelation" and "the natural knowledge of God." And after everything that has been discovered and formulated, we cannot simply take over the insights of Kraemer and van der Leeuw, either. The situation is made even more difficult for the dogmatician because the current dominant trend in the science of religion does not run to fundamental, so much as to empirical, questions. The intent of scholars is to understand religious people and their ideas in, and sometimes in terms of, their social, political, and economic ties or contexts. Earlier generations rarely bothered themselves with these factors. A "catchup" maneuver in this area, achieved largely by way of such other disciplines as sociology, is therefore necessary. Unfortunately, this need coincides with the necessity, in dogmatic studies, to undertake a similar "catchup" by way of the history of religion. The material it is looking for in connection with the question of truth is even scarcer now.

At this time the dogmatician cannot operate without a certain acquaintance at least with Judaism, Hinduism, and Islam. This is necessary not only in the interest of interpreting the gospel in our pluralistic and multireligious society but also because of the challenge and allure of these religions. We cannot speak of "revelation" anymore without asking why and in what respect the Surahs of the Koran must, or must not, be regarded as revelation from the same God. And we can no longer speak of "salvation" without asking whether the Indian notion of "bhakti" relates to the love of the God of Jesus as reflection or as contradiction.

It used to be that churches, without much knowledge, dismissed testimonies from the world of the religions as the work of the devil. Today many Christians, again without much knowledge, assume that all religions have more or less the same meaning as the Christian faith. The dogmatician who believes that in Christ "all the treasures of wisdom and knowledge are hidden" (Col. 2:3) and that God "did not leave himself without witness" (Acts 14:17) to the nations around the world will listen to the testimonies of world religions with a receptive mind and hope that by doing so he will gain, whether by their contribution or by their contradiction, a deeper understanding and interpretation of salvation in Christ. Perhaps, as a result, he will acquire such an all-embracing view of the phenomena of the religions that as a subdivision of his dogmatics he will be emboldened to construct a *theologia religionum*. But it is a question whether that really belongs to his department of study. In any case, for this purpose, one has to have exceptionally good scientific credentials. Another question is whether dogmatics could not well serve the science of religion in the definition of its foundational concepts (such as "revelation") and in the search for a principle of organization (e.g., polytheism *vs.* monotheism, naturalistic *vs.* prophetic religions). But that issue falls outside the scope of this section.

4.6 DOGMATICS AND ETHICS

If dogmatics is scientific reflection on the Christian faith, then ethics is scientific reflection on believing action. It is clear, therefore, that here we are only talking about Christian ethics. Other systems of ethics exist, and at some state universities there is, within the department of theology, a field of study called *Ethics* that is closely allied to the philosophy of religion. There are different approaches to this field of study; sometimes it is conceived as an attempt to construct a "general" ethics, and nowadays also as "metaethics," that is, research in the presuppositions in terms of which a given course of action can be called good or bad. Christian ethics undertakes to think about the specific action that is based on the premises of the Christian faith. And since it belongs to those premises to say that faith and action are intimately bound up with each other, it is clear that dogmatics and ethics have a great deal to do with each other. This relationship is at least as close as that between dogmatics and the study of the Old and the New Testament or that between dogmatics and church history. But it is of a different kind. Dogmatics is not dependent on the results of ethics in the same way that it is dependent on the results of these two other fields of study. The reverse, however, is true: the examination of the action of faith is also dependent on the results of research in the content of faith. In redemptive revelation God approaches us with the intent to involve us in it so that we, in our conduct, begin to conform to it. But when we formulate the matter thus it is clear that dogmatics can no more dissociate itself from ethics than ethics can dissociate itself from dogmatics. Salvation aims at the renewal of our being and, therefore, of our action; it cannot be defined apart from the purpose intended. Thus, no part of dogmatics is without ethical implications. And in the subdivision that concerns itself particularly with the realization of salvation in human life (in classic terminology it is called "soteriology"), it is inevitable that even systematic theology would concern itself explicitly with the foundations of ethics, certainly in the discussions of renewal after the image of Christ and the love of God and neighbor. On the subject of the foundations of ethics the dogmatician and the ethicist will have to consult each other frequently. But the elaboration of those themes and their application in a number of different spheres and in relation to current problems is entirely the province of ethics as a field of study that logically follows that of dogmatics.

In his letter to the Galatians Paul speaks in a striking phrase of "faith working through love" (5:6). That gives expression both to a certain sequence and to an unbreakable unity. In many of his letters he starts out with the content of the faith and concentrates in the second place on the Christian conduct of life. There is distinction, not separation. Theology later often embroidered on that frame, making a distinction, for example, between "credenda" and "agenda." It was especially due to Melanchthon's influence that this split between dogmatics and ethics was carried out and carried on. That is equivalent to saying that in preceding centuries another relationship was predominant. The phrase "faith working through love," after all, can with equal justice be read as speaking of the unity of the two as of their distinction. It is for that reason that Augustine, in his small dogmatic handbook the *Enchiridion*, weaves ethics into dogmatics. In Thomas Aquinas the doctrine concerning the duties, virtues, and vices fills the largest part of the very long *Secunda secundae* (II.2) of the *Summa Theologica*. In the *Institutes*, Calvin offers an extensive exposition of the decalogue (II.8) and later treats the Christian life (III.6-10). Also in more recent times ethics was incorporated into dogmatics. An example is that of Martin Kähler's *Die Wissenschaft der Christlichen Lehre* (1883), which consists of three parts: apologetics, dogmatics, and ethics. But the best-known example comes from Karl Barth, who treats ethics as a part of, or, rather, as a series of parts of, his *Church Dogmatics*. In support of this he reasons that a division of dogmatics and ethics entails a double danger. On the one hand, dogmatics becomes abstract since it is divorced from its ethical intent; on the other hand, ethics threatens to be based on something other than redemptive revelation — on anthropology, for example, or on natural law, or on conservative or revolutionary principles.

There is a third way of reading Paul's statement concerning "faith working through love": namely, that only the act or practice of love constitutes the realization of faith, hence, a working faith is always a kind of "praxis." On that view the ethical precedes the doctrinal, and believing action has to be seen as *one,* if not *the,* fount of knowledge concerning that which dogmatics has to formulate as being saving reality. Dogmatics, then, has to be viewed as "critical reflection on human action." This view of the relationship between dogmatics and ethics arose around 1965 and has since gained much ground. Currently there is a variety of dogmatic thought-forms taking their point of departure in "the praxis of liberating action" and seeking to define anew the content of the faith in terms of the experiences gained in this praxis. We have in mind "the theology of revolution," "political theology," "black theology," and "feminist theology." The best-known form of it is "liberation theology" as it was developed in Latin America. Its classic statement is that of Gustavo Gutiérrez, *A Theology of Liberation* (Orbis, 1973), in which he justifies this mode of theologizing (see I.B). It is too early to tell whether this praxis-based dogmatic reflection will yield lasting returns. It would seem to me that the question whether — and if so, then how far — dogmatics can derive its inspiration from a liberation praxis is a question that needs to be resolved in advance and is itself a dogmatic question that, like all dogmatic questions, needs to be settled vis-à-vis redemptive revelation.

However the answer to the question of the relationship between dogmatics and ethics is formulated, the issue itself has been virtually decided almost everywhere in favor of the first of the three positions sketched here. The curricula at our theological schools and seminaries recognize dogmatics and ethics as two distinct disciplines that, moreover, are rarely taught by one person. Yet even with this arrangement the second and third positions can be honored in part, such as by professors establishing parallel themes and working together. When I say "in part" I have in mind particularly the fact that as a result of macroethical convulsions since World War II the subject matter covered in ethics has expanded enormously and, in addition, cannot be managed without a certain amount of acquaintance with sociology, social psychology, economics, political science, polemology (nuclear movement!), and more. It is impossible to bring all this material together within the scope of dogmatics. For that matter, in Barth it is already evident that the ethical sections bring with them a method of their own, the result being that their connection with the dogmatic material turns out to be less direct than was announced. This is clear particularly in the solidly ethical *Church Dogmatics* III/4. It must be possible even in an independent study of ethics to keep in view, as foundation and norm, the faith that works through love.

4.7 DOGMATICS AND PRACTICAL THEOLOGY

On this relationship we can be more brief. Here, the same applies, in principle, as what was said about the relationship between dogmatics and Christian ethics. One could even consider practical theology a division of ethics. In both instances we are concerned with the norms for Christian action. Practical theology then investigates the norms for action within the church as institution, especially as regards its official functions: worship, proclamation, catechesis, pastoral care, building up the church. As a rule, however, practical theology tends to occupy a much larger place in the theological education than ethics. There it functions as the professional training of pastors. For a long time ethics, situated between dogmatics and practical theology, played only a minor role in many schools of theology. Since the Second World War, and particularly since around 1965, that role has become increasingly larger. In the process, a combination of ethics with (parts of) practical theology has become rare.

In addition to its methodological link with ethics, practical theology has its kinship with dogmatics, one that concerns partly method and partly content. Its work presupposes dogmatics. Just as dogmatics borders on the philosophy of religion in its prolegomena, on New Testament scholarship in its Christology, and on ethics in its doctrine of sanctification, so it borders on practical theology in its doctrine of the church. In each of these cases, for that matter, one could better speak of "overlapping with" than of "bordering on." In the case of practical theology, one has to add that the dogmatician, in his work, aims also and sometimes primarily at giving inspiration and direction to pastors in their work. It is not strange, therefore, that a good number of professors in practical theology took their doctorates in dogmatics.

Just as is the case with ethics, the traffic between dogmatics and practical theology sometimes goes both ways. For dogmatics relates to the present-day life of the churches as one of its areas of experience, which is precisely that area to which practical theology directs its critical attention. This critical reflection can help dogmatics to refine or adjust *its* concepts. Dogmatics, after all, occupies itself with the process of transmitting salvation to people. For practical theology that process by itself is the entire object of its critical reflection. Dogmatics is primarily focused on salvation itself and on the transmission of it from the salvation perspective. Within the context of this concern the human person who receives salvation may easily remain somewhat in the shadows. The opposite danger looms in practical theology: in large tracts of its literature today it seems as if that person with his experiences and wishes has the first and the last word, so that he determines and restricts salvation. Both disciplines, then, need to complement and correct each other.

More important, as we have remarked before, the dogmatician himself must continue to take part in the actual life and work of the church. When he preaches regularly and takes part in catechesis and training sessions, the questions with which he struggles in his study strike him in still a very different way. It was the experience of being unable, in face-to-face contact with catechumens, to establish an existential link between them and the classical doctrines of the Trinity and election that led me years ago to search for other ways to present these points in dogmatics. I believe it was the German philosopher Kamlah who remarked that the sermons of the great church fathers and of the Reformers open up dogmatic perspectives that are far richer than those of their official dogmatic treatises. The pastorate causes the dogmatician to discover (to his horror) how many answers he knows to questions no one (any longer) asks, and how few answers he has at his disposal when people confront him with questions concerning providence and suffering. All this, when all is well, affects the way he does theology.

These examples show how fruitful it can be to shift back from the practice of the church to dogmatics. That is not identical with shifting back from practical theology to dogmatics; but the dogmatician may assume that when he starts thinking from a vantage point in the practice of the church, practical theology has already done this earlier and more extensively than he, and so he will be able to profit from discussions and results in this neighboring discipline. This seems to me especially imperative in ecclesiology. Ecclesiology still suffers in dogmatics from a high degree of abstractness. The church discussed in ecclesiology often seems to have little to do with the actual church in which we exist and which we form. Under the circumstances, the practical theologian will have to trouble the dogmatician with hard questions — also with material from his ancillary sources, like sociology. He has all the more reason for doing it since it is the dogmatician's job to offer him a blueprint of ecclesiology with which he can work. Conversely, the dogmatician may and must, if necessary, trouble the practical theologian with the question of whether he is not too exclusively oriented to experience and is doing justice to the Spirit who is the actual secret of this life.

4.8 THE MODERN DOGMATICIAN AS DILETTANTE AND SYMPHONY DIRECTOR

This heading is a quotation, which has become a rather well-known saying, of the title of an oration with which the dogmatician K. H. Miskotte took leave, in 1959, of his academic post in Leiden. As I look back toward the preceding sections of this fourth chapter, I see the dogmatician standing, amid the other theological disciplines, in precisely this paradoxical double role. He needs the help of many other sciences as a nonexpert in these fields. He needs to master their methods and findings, in the main, through personal contacts and consultations, and by reading more or less comprehensive works. In all this he is doomed to remain a dilettante, vulnerable to the varied criticisms of specialists. Miskotte mentions the "extraordinary weariness" that is the outcome of all this. But he realizes that it is the flip side of a different kind of calling, one that is comparable to that of the symphony director. That designation may sound a trifle arrogant. Miskotte resists the accusation by pointing out, on the one hand, that the director must himself be able to make music, "being versed in two leading instruments which are dominant in a modern orchestra" (from an incidental reference it is clear he has in mind exegesis and the history of dogma); on the other hand, he stresses that the director is no more than a performing artist, and is strictly bound to the score, in this case the Word of God.

What Miskotte here playfully, yet profoundly, puts into words, I should like to illumine with another image. In one way or another all scholarship and science must serve society and culture in their journey through history. The service rendered by theology consists in bringing up for discussion, and keeping on the human agenda, the subject of God — God in his relationship and relevance to man. It is not necessary for specialists in the different nondogmatic disciplines to think every moment of that ultimate goal; it is better even if they do not (see conclusion of 2.6). But anyone who is not a specialist in the narrow sense will think of it repeatedly. So when he offers the results of his study to a broader reading circle, he will find the conceptual material of dogmatics indispensable. Then he has a choice; not between dogmatics and no dogmatics, but between a worse and a better dogmatics.

Now for the image. We can view each of these disciplines as a region around a railway station from which trains regularly leave, transporting the products of that region to the consumers. On this route the trains will always have to pass by the station of dogmatics, the point of trans-shipment where the products are graded and regrouped. Now without the imagery: the results of dogmatics must be so formulated that they can serve as elements of the answer people look for in their quest for God. I am not saying that the dogmatician must dictate his answer to his fellow theologians. A person must not let himself be guided by one person any more in the dogmatic arena than in other fields. But why should the specialist himself not put into words the final questions and answers of his specialty? Only he must then realize that he is now about to sit on a chair other than his own, a chair on which *he* is a dilettante. The best way to proceed is with cooperation between specialists from the different disciplines. In such a framework the dogmatician can then function as chairman, that is, as the one who patiently listens to all sides, who sometimes makes his contribution as a participant in the discussion, and whose duty it is finally to formulate the outcome in the form of policy decisions, so that it can begin to be effective in the outside world.

Five

DOGMATICS IN TIME AND SPACE

5.1 IS THERE DEVELOPMENT IN DOGMATICS?

Dogmatics is a fairly ancient science: not as ancient as philosophy, history, or astronomy, but much older than most sciences now taught at our universities. It is also a science that has been pursued, in the course of its history, in very diverse cultures. And in our century, if not before, it is pursued in almost the entire world in very many cultural contexts. This field of study, therefore, has great length in time and is now gaining great width in space. Both of these facts confront us with questions that are themselves of a dogmatic nature. In 5.1 and 5.2 we shall touch upon the questions that relate to the aspect of time; in 5.3 and 5.4 we shall deal with questions that arise from the spatial dimension.

Now that dogmatic theology has been done for nineteen centuries, there is good reason to survey this work as a historic whole and to ask ourselves whether clear lines of development can be discerned in it. We do have to remember that this question itself can arise only in a culture that has learned to think historically and then in terms of development. That is the case in general only in European – North American culture since around 1800. This way of thinking is especially suited to the so-called

57

exact sciences, in which succeeding researchers always build on the achievements of their predecessors and in which, when great creative or revolutionary leaps occur (as achieved by Copernicus, Newton, Darwin, and Einstein), the earlier results are incorporated and carried forward as now relativized elements or foundations in the new thought-models. In these fields of study knowledge of the history of the field is useful but not essential to the average practitioner.

The situation is very different in the classic studies. Philosophy, as an adjacent area, affords a clear illustration of this. No one will say that Plato and Aristotle have been made "obsolete" by medieval scholasticism, German Idealism, or American process philosophy. Philosophical connoisseurs have said that modern philosophy has done little else than write footnotes to the Greek. And someone like Heidegger deliberately reaches back to the earliest phase of that philosophy (the pre-Socratics) because he believes that is when the fundamental questions were posed and best answered. In general one can say that those branches of study that occupy themselves with man, and specifically those that occupy themselves with the universe, with being, or with God, cannot develop in a straight line. The object of their study and reflection is so inexhaustible that the "advance" of these disciplines (which differs from "progress") consists in the continual discovery of new elements in the object. It is as if in the course of centuries, there is a circular procession around the object in order to discover in it, each time from another vantage point in history or experience in culture, aspects that escaped earlier generations or struck them differently.

This reasoning applies with even greater force to dogmatics as the science concerning the self-revealing God. For its object it has, in an absolute sense, the inexhaustible; indeed, the Inexhaustible. For that reason it is caught up in a never-ending process — which is less a progression than a procession. One can hardly say that Aquinas rendered Augustine out-of-date, or that Schleiermacher made Luther obsolete. Is there, then, no progress in this process at all? Are there no insights and results that later centuries can simply take for granted?

In the nineteenth century some, under the influence of Hegel and subsequent thought in terms of organism and evolution, believed they could observe a development in the history of theology. The Anglican (and later Roman Catholic) theologian John Henry Newman wrote "An Essay on the Development of Christian Doctrine" (1845), in which he "demonstrated" that the doctrinal content of the Christian church unfolded in a straight line and completely maintained its identity from its origin to the Roman Catholic doctrine of his own time. The Lutheran theologian Gottfried Thomasius, in his *Die christliche Dogmengeschichte als Entwicklungsgeschichte des kirchlichen Lehrbegriffs"* (1874 – 1876), saw how initially the Greeks developed the doctrine concerning God and his triunity and that concerning the person of Christ; next how the North Africans (Romans) developed the doctrines concerning man and his sin; after that how the Medievalists developed the doctrine concerning the work of Christ (the Atonement); and finally how the Reformers developed the doctrine concerning the appropriation of salvation (justification). The culmination and terminus of this development is then attained in the Lutheran confessions.

A much more cautious and somewhat more complex model, constructed under the influence of the *Wesensschau* (intuition of essence) of phenomenology, is offered by Noordmans in his study *Het Kerkelijk Dogma* (1934), in which he distinguishes between three phases of dogmatic development: the symbolic or speculative (the Greeks); the rhetorical, or sacramental, or semi-Pelagian (the Romans and the Medievalists); and the pastoral, in which doctrine is directed entirely toward personal application (the Reformers and Karl Barth).

Nowadays we regard such all-embracing schemes very skeptically. It would seem that no one can map out such developments without seeing himself more or less at the end of it all. It is therefore better not to speak of progress. It is repeatedly the experience of scholars that someone before us already observed what *we* thought was an original discovery, and sometimes this earlier scholar dug considerably deeper, and formulated his findings more strikingly, than we did.

So, although we cannot really speak of progress (since for that purpose we lack a suprahistorical standpoint and hence a standard), we do have to speak, on account of the many twists and turns in the history of theology, of a process — a restless process even, one that often entails a return to earlier insights, be it never entirely from the same perspective. We need to ask, What is the dynamic force behind that process? Is that the Spirit who leads us in all truth? But the first thing that strikes us is the connection between that dynamic force and the changes in the general cultural situations in which the dogmaticians find themselves. Every cultural period is centered around experiences and discoveries that lead to the formation of a certain sense of life. Churches and their dogmaticians participate in that sense. From within that sense of life they regard the sources of faith and theology with eyes different from their predecessors'. Certain favorite and central Bible passages lose their expressiveness; other passages, neglected or ill-understood until now, suddenly claim the limelight.

The dogmatician, more than he realizes, receives his inspiration from the time in which he lives. But his loyalty is on the side of the gospel. That gospel seeks to address and renew the people of every period. That address also, if not especially, proceeds by way of contradiction. Both as a believer and as a professional theologian the dogmatician has to deal with two of Paul's statements. The first is ". . . I have made myself a slave to all, that I might win the more. To the Jews I became as a Jew, in order to win Jews. . . . To the weak I became weak, that I might win the weak. I have become all things to all men, that I might by all means save some" (1 Cor. 9:19ff.). But also: ". . . we preach Christ crucified, a stumbling block to Jews and folly to Gentiles, but to those who are called, both Jews and Greeks, Christ the power of God and the wisdom of God" (1 Cor. 1:23-24). From the tension between these two statements the gospel is transposed, in all the changes of culture, into ever new semantic fields, not in order to accommodate it to the spirit of the times but to call one's contemporaries to conversion and liberation in the idiom and concepts of their time.

Christian thinkers rooted in a preceding period are often repelled by the changes in language, understanding, and perspective of the present. They miss so much of that which means a lot to them and find much of what is currently central incomprehensible and even unacceptable. For a few decades the succeeding generation cannot dialogue with these predecessors. It frequently feels more attracted to the thinking of the *pre*-preceding generation against which the preceding one rebelled. With the onset of a new sense of life in the cultural consciousness, there arises . . . etc.

The history of dogmatic thought is replete with unexpected turns and breaks. In the last two centuries they seem to succeed each other even more quickly than before. One may wish to keep his distance from them but usually that is because one is stuck in an earlier phase. And yet, a theologian may never climb aboard current bandwagons — a point we shall discuss in the next section. But neither can he place himself outside his own time. For it is his task intellectually to think through the Christian faith with a view to his own time. He must maintain his stance in the tension between the two statements of Paul cited above. But he must not be so naive as to think that he is a better interpreter of the gospel than a predecessor in the fourth or sixteenth century. Most of the theological works of the present will be unreadable in just a few decades. And the great theologians of the past will always be read again and prove inspiring. One is well-advised, in dogmatic matters, not to say too quickly that something is "outdated." Let us rather be modest and say that we in our time, given our responsibilities for this time, see no way of integrating the truth of that "something." Nothing that springs from the depth of the gospel is ever out-of-date. But it sometimes has to wait a long time before it is operative again.

So then there is no progress in dogmatics, is there? Only an erratic and discontinuous back-and-forth movement? But this is an incorrect set of alternatives. Always and everywhere we theologize in the terms of the gospel that keeps us together and at least makes the dialogue or dispute between us possible. And we may believe that the Holy Spirit leads us in all truth *through* this restless process of trial and error, of dead-ends and open roads. But that leading takes place in response to ever-changing challenges and from ever-different points of entry. Whether this process constitutes progress is something that can only be known *sub specie aeternitatis*. We simply cannot view things from a vantage point in eternity but always have to struggle along in time.

5.2 DATED OR ETERNAL?

At the end of the previous section we encountered certain profound questions. We must continue that discussion for a moment. We shall tie it in with that last statement: we do not find ourselves in eternity but take part in time. This is true; but we already heard that in our own time we have to represent the supratemporal perspectives and powers of the gospel. Our stance is in time. And in time we face eternity. These two are not mutually exclusive. The core of the gospel is precisely that the Word becomes flesh — which also means that the Word assumed the shape of our history, himself becoming history. The Word became a Jewish man, who acted in public at the time of Emperor Tiberius. Eternity expresses itself in calendar dates.

For the natural or philosophic mind this is a cross: *the* paradox, it is also subject to it. This is especially true since around A.D. 1800. In 5.1 we noted that from that time on intellectual pioneers began to think in fundamental, historical terms. In the preceding "Christian centuries" people lived by eternal and unchangeably fixed truths that are not subject to time and apply despite the changes in it. On that point philosophy and theology were agreed. It is likely that people at that time also had much less feeling for the twists and turns of history in a cultural sense. European intellectuals felt a kinship with the classics of Greco-Roman antiquity that was nearly as close as that with their own intellectual contemporaries. Admittedly, in dogmatics one could say things in a manner different from one's predecessors, but that was because at certain points they were either heretical or illogical. Every serious dogmatician assumed he was writing something that could endure throughout the ages because it expressed that which was always true. When the Reformers suddenly began to formulate things very differently, that had nothing to do, to their way of thinking, with advance in time or progress in their cultures; they "only" meant to bring the eternal truth of the gospel out from under its human encrustations and malformations.

The Lutheran theologian and philosopher of Romanticism, Johann Gottfried Herder (1744 – 1803), can be viewed as the first to apply the notion of "development" to theology. To him everything is embedded in history, hence dated, relativized, and conditioned by that which preceded it. And probably the first dogmatician to consider his own approach as dated is Schleier- macher: on the one hand, he wanted to respond to the rise of secularization; and, on the other, he sought to offer a theological foundation to the union of the Lutherans and the Reformed, which took definite form in Prussia in those years.

Since then the feeling that dogmaticians do not write for all time but for their own time has become almost universal. The result of this is that now we can also tell how dated earlier theologians were in their analysis and formulation. Augustine gave the Christian answer to the Platonizing sense of life that characterized the Roman empire in its final stages. Thomas Aquinas, who made Aristotle into a servant of supernatural truth, by this means built his defenses against Averroism, the first wave of secularization that washed over the European church and culture. And the Reformation, which only wanted to put the full light of the gospel on the church's candlestick, with its emphasis on personal faith, was simultaneously the answer to the rising need for the personalization of life and culture as it came to forceful expression in the late Middle Ages, in the Ren- aissance, and in Humanism. Calvin's *Institutes* is not conceiv- able apart from the rise of Humanism. And the conflict between Arminians and Calvinists, between Jansenists and Jesuits, is un- thinkable apart from the trends toward internalization and au- tonomy in the emerging Baroque period.

But that which happened unconsciously at that time has increasingly been a conscious goal in the nineteenth and the twentieth centuries. An exception seems to be the theology of Karl Barth, although its emergence as a protest in the name of God against the anthropocentric bourgeois culture of Europe was very much dated in the early years of confusion and reflec- tion following the First World War.

In the present period the urge to produce timely and rele- vant theology has reached a zenith. Many scholars are so eager to do their theologizing vis-à-vis the themes of our time (such as "revolution," "liberation," "emancipation") that they make the gospel into a confirmation if not an echo of answers already available in the culture apart from the gospel. The task of playing a contrapuntal melody on behalf of the gospel, a task with which dogmatics stands or falls, has then been given up. Datedness has then swallowed up permanence. It is true that real dogmatics must be willing to — in fact, must — enter upon a discussion of all these questions. But it must not, in meeting the challenges, be totally absorbed by them, because the answers come from the Word that transcends, delimits, and transforms our questions. It is to this conflictual and liberating encounter between the Word and the questions arising from our sense of our present situation in life that dogmatics has to be serviceable. This means that dogmatics, while giving datedness and relevance its due, has to make room for the preponderance of eternity. All present-day concepts must be forged in the direction of Christ. To do the reverse is to betray the dogmatician's mandate.

Still, actuality and eternity must walk side by side in dogmatic thought. But how can they? The dogmatician who, because the *Word* became *flesh,* takes the conjunction of the two seriously, knows where his limits lie but can still take one of two directions. We may mention two extremes; at the first, the dogmatician can position himself at the periphery of dogmatics, the point where it borders on apologetics and ethics, and construct, for example, a "dogmatics of liberation," taking his point of departure in the present-day longing for liberation, relating it next to what salvation and redemption mean in the gospel, and finally returning to our concept of liberation in order to correct and deepen it. At the other extreme, the dogmatician can take his position at the center of his discipline, developing the key words of the Christian faith with rigor, in terms of their own content and coherence, not worrying about the question of how they finally "land." Both methods are legitimate but each has a price tag. The first approach will find a ready and wide hearing and help people in their actual situation, but after ten years it will probably be forgotten. The second, because it lacks contemporary relevance, runs the risk of getting little attention; but if the work is deep enough and is well written it may have grateful readers in several successive periods, readers who though they do not find their own questions explictly formulated in it will find the answers to their questions there. Only works of this second group are likely ever to be counted among the classics.

Our conclusion is impossible to avoid: the advantage of the first category is that it has current pastoral effectiveness; the advantage of the second is that it has the power of historical influence, a power that comes repeatedly to expression in new periods. The work of the first period of the Reformation, especially that of Luther and Calvin, has a high grade of supratemporal power. This seems also to be true of the later works of Karl Barth. Such works never become totally timeless but because of their evangelical depth remain readable in all times. We can also mention here the name of Herman Bavinck, although it was his conscious wish to be much closer to his own times than the others we have mentioned. And it is exactly those parts of his work in which he tried hard to be relevant that now strike us as antiquated and largely unintelligible.

Both genres, then, have their place and we would not want to be without either of them. Whatever and however we write, we always date ourselves. Because of the Word which became flesh, this is a fact we may accept as self-evident; indeed, we must view it as a duty we owe our neighbor, the church, and the world around us, which we seek to serve with our theologizing. But the dangers loom larger to the extent that we strive more consciously to be relevant. The thing we need consciously to strive for is to interpret the gospel. And because we ourselves are dated, this datedness will probably always be noticeable — we may hope to the benefit of many readers.

A beginner in this study of dogmatics is often fascinated by strongly dated dogmatic writings. Such writings provide the initial impetus, open up perspectives, and set us in motion. Therein lies their value and justification. But the time comes when they lose their lustre and we in turn want to get to a higher level where the "eternal weight" of the object of this discipline makes itself felt so much more forcefully. It is in these higher regions that our field of study comes fully into its own.

5.3 THE GEOGRAPHY AND SOCIOGRAPHY OF DOGMATICS

After dealing with the problems posed by the dimension of time in our dogmatic endeavors, we now turn to the problems that arise from the spread in space: the fact that the systematic labor of interpreting the gospel takes place among a great variety of peoples, languages, and cultures. Space, like time, confronts dogmatics with dogmatic questions. But these questions are, in part, of the same nature: How far must we, in our theologizing, let ourselves be determined by our situation — whether it be a phase or sphere of culture? Further, to a significant extent both types of questions coincide because the study of theology took place successively in different cultural spheres: the Greek-Hellenistic, the Roman, the Latin-European, the German-European, and (partly parallel to this latter one) the European – Anglo-Saxon, and the American (predominantly Anglo-Saxon). For a number of these viewpoints we therefore have to refer to 5.1 and 5.2. The present section, 5.3, is the spatial parallel to 5.1. The spatial dimension as such, however, demands another viewpoint, a contemporary geographic perspective on this discipline and its history; in this connection certain sociographic views will fit in naturally.

Until very recently dogmatics was a European – North American enterprise, pursued mainly at universities, theological schools, and seminaries. This pursuit spread to the Third World by way of various missions, but instructors there were Westerners or at least were trained in the West, so that no significant native contributions could be expected from these regions. In the Second World, Eastern Orthodox theology has been forced by communism into a very restricted area where it can do little else than move in traditional channels. The theology of Russian émigrés (with its centers in Paris and New York), in its interaction with the West, has, however, produced a remarkable and surprising reinterpretation, but one that is not accepted in the motherland.

Spain, Italy, and France have been dominant in Roman Catholic dogmatics. It is in these countries that the theology of the Roman Curia — counter-Reformation and neo-Thomistic — originated. France offered certain daring and influential exceptions, especially after 1930 when the "nouvelle theologie" arose. Catholic theology in Germany and England tended to be freer, partly as a result of its relationship with the surrounding Protestantism. Following the Second Vatican Council this greater flexibility in European Catholic theology became so general that in method and content it could often hardly be distinguished from Protestant theology. While confessional differences are growing blurred (within Protestantism as well), geographic, linguistic, and national differences still prove to be very strong.

In the Netherlands, oriented as it is to German and English, we become especially sensitive to the difference between the Anglo-Saxon and German way of doing theology. In the nature of the case, we can only characterize that difference by making broad generalizations and ignoring exceptions or nuances. With these reservations in mind we can say that German dogmatic literature addresses all problems both very fundamentally (*grundsätzlich*) and very thoroughly (*gründlich*) and is highly abstract. The descriptive is overshadowed by the speculative. This mode of thinking and writing is often appropriately paired with a difficult, laborious, and obscure mode of expression: "Why put it simply when you can also say it in a complicated way?" English dogmaticians, on the other hand, often write in a nearly conversational style, one that is full of understatements, and stay as long as they can on a (historical) descriptive plane. Where the German way borders on the metaphysical and philosophic, the Anglo-Saxon borders on that of the history of theology and culture. While the Germans in their theologizing have to come to terms with Kant, Hegel, Husserl, and Heidegger, the English are conditioned in their way of thinking by Hume, Wittgenstein, positivism, and the language-analysis school of philosophy. American theology is predominantly Anglo-Saxon, very pragmatic, and especially in dialogue with psychology and sociology, both of them the products of modernity. The Americans are less exclusive in their orientation than the British, and very open to the continental-European insights that they then proceed to assimilate independently. (The Germans, for that matter, are as exclusive as the British.) The difference in language and cultural atmosphere is such that often people of the one culture only half understand those of the other. A typical example of this was the controversy between Barth and Brunner in 1934 concerning the question of whether there is in man an *Anknüpfungspunkt* (point of contact) for God's grace. Their disagreement parted European theologians into two camps that passionately opposed each other. But in England (much less in Scotland) scholars looked on this controversy with detachment and semi-boredom. And in America the joke went around that "there cannot be much difference between Barth and Brunner, because they both believe in God!" These divergent reactions were due, in large part, to the fact that to German ears *Anknüpfungspunkt* is a loaded term, almost a metaphysical expression reminiscent of synergism and Pelagianism, whereas the English phrase "point of contact" expresses something pragmatic and self-evident.

French-language theology with its Latinate lucidity stands off to one side a bit — often consciously and with a touch of hauteur. But its radius of influence is smaller than that of the other two modern languages. Nor must German-language Swiss theology be confused with the German. It expresses itself in much clearer and more sober terms without, however, becoming Anglo-Saxon. Its dogmatics tends to regard biblical theology as its closest neighbor. And Dutch dogmatics? Generally, it feels itself akin to the Swiss way of thinking, in any case considerably more than to the Anglo-Saxon. We are deterred, in German theology, by the metaphysical and absolute; in the British by the predominantly empirical and its relativizing tendency; in the ("liberal") American theological world by the dominance of frequently secularistic concepts borrowed from other disciplines. At the same time we feel that all three traditions offer indispensable viewpoints by which they exert a sound relativizing and correcting influence on each other.

As a "delta-culture" the Netherlands is open, theologically as well as culturally, in every direction, and because of its language orientation it is especially open toward the East and the West. In being broadly receptive to influences from other language-areas we are equalled only perhaps by the Swiss and the Scandinavians, among whom we are surpassed by the Finns. That effect may be negative or positive: negative when it produces a feeling of inferiority, which leads to eclecticism and syncretism; positive when it stimulates our creativity and leads to syntheses. Whatever belongs to the first kind generally remains unknown outside our borders; a fair amount of material of the second kind has been translated, especially after the war, into German and English (much less into French). It is owing to this fact—therefore not altogether justly—that Dutch theology enjoys a very good reputation, which does not mean it is read very much. We might well be more conscious of our intermediate position between languages and cultures in order, through our publications, to bring within each other's hearing regions that often lie far apart.

This, until recently, is how the geography of the dogmatic enterprise looked. This is still how it looks, but there is more to say. Other regions, also other groups within the regions we have mentioned, are busy conquering their place in dogmatics by storm. The most ancient credentials belong to the theology of India, Roman Catholic theology as well as Protestant. In that country theology is done vis-à-vis an overwhelming Hindu culture, and for that reason it is done with an unusual (by comparison with our traditions) and almost heretical-sounding emphasis on the mystical, cosmic, and universal aspects of the gospel. Other Asiatic theologies (Japan, Indonesia) remain closer to Western patterns of thought. In newly independent African states, with their preoccupation with nation building and identity, the attempt is made to bend the gospel as far as possible in the direction of ancient tribal religions with their "primal visions." At present there is a mighty upsurge in dogmatic activity in Latin America. Its roots lie in Western Europe and in North America, among both Catholics and Protestants, but it is developed, with or without the aid of Marxist ideas, in the face of the situation of exploitation that prevails there. For the context of these new theologies and their interconnection with feminist and black theology, I wish to refer to the concluding pages of 3.4.

As a result of this rapid geographic expansion into very different cultures, our "Western" dogmatics begins to look different. It is no longer alone; nor is it the only valid one. We have become conscious of its cultural conditioning and limits. What that means for the question of truth, we will discuss in 5.4.

In the World Council of Churches in particular this explosion of new and newly situated theologies in the Third World has led, in the sixties and seventies, to many dialogues and clashes. Sometimes it looked as if mutual recognition and kinship would be lost in the process and that every cultural region would retreat to its own mode of doing theology. The mission conference in Bangkok (1973), for example, almost turned into a Babel of confusion. Still, the joy of seeing everyone interpreting the mighty works of God, or of hearing them interpreted in one's own language, should make us think of a new Pentecost. How that could and should happen will be treated in 5.4. We do want to report here that after Bangkok there was the clear start of a countermovement in which, from the base of the one gospel as point of reference, a search was conducted for what we hold in common.

Finally, let me say a word on what is called "sociography" in the title of this section. Who are the bearers of dogmatic theology and in what particular life-situation is it produced? In antiquity the bishops usually were driven to do theology under pressure from recalcitrant heretics. This changed in the thirteenth century with the rise of the universities where "doctores," very often monks belonging to the Dominican or Franciscan orders, developed their views and systems. Since the Renaissance and the secularization of the universities that came with it, the Roman Catholic Church withdrew, by preference, into seminaries or Catholic universities; dogmatics is developed there and in monasteries predominantly by members of monastic orders. Protestants did involve themselves with modern universities where this was possible (as in the Netherlands). Among them it is especially the professors of theology who carry the dogmatic enterprise forward. This may lead to a measure of estrangement from the churches — a real tendency, especially in Germany. But tension between church and theology is by no means absent in places where the instructors have closer ties with the churches, as in most North American seminaries. This is because dogmatics is increasingly practiced, transconfessionally, by the same rules (see 3.3). As theological and ecumenical contacts broaden, tension with one's own tradition may the more easily run high.

As a result of the geographic expansion of the practice of dogmatic theology into the Third World, its social base of operation is broadened. This is also happening, for that matter, in the First World. Today in addition to professors, preachers, and priests, nontheological intellectuals, groups promoting black consciousness, feminist movements, and especially base communities, oppressed and exploited or not, have begun to take part in the theological dialogue. This broadening of participation is an entirely new, and much to be welcomed, development. We shall deal with its perils and possibilities in the following section.

5.4 CONTEXTUALITY OR UNIVERSAL VALIDITY?

Just as 5.1 ended with the fundamental problem discussed in 5.2, so 5.3 has to end with a similar problem, posed now not with reference to successive phases in time but with reference to a wide spread in space. Growing self-awareness in the Third World (symptomatic of which in Christian churches is a distrust of Western theology) has led in these churches to a demand for the "contextualization" of dogmatics: people no longer wish to be guided by Western concepts and definitions of problems but by the problems and ideals that prevail in their own land, race, class, and culture.

The cry for contextualization, which repels so many Western (northern) theologians, is to be taken seriously, if for no other reason than that it enables us to become conscious of the extent to which our own theological practice is shaped and colored by our European – North American culture. That is true not only for our present practice but has been true for centuries, as it was true for the preceding stages of dogmatic study: the Jewish-Christian, the Hellenistic, and the late Roman. The cry from other places for contextual theology makes us conscious of our own contextuality. It enables us to see how, from the time of Augustine via the Reformation and Pietism to Bultmann and his school, our theological attention has been directed toward the salvation of the individual. In our day, a time of secularization and prosperity, that pursuit has narrowed down to the question of the meaning of the life of the individual. (We have solved other questions or they do not interest us.) But in most other regions of the world life is lived and experienced on a more elementary plane and in a more collective setting. Our interpretation of the gospel, from their point of view, often seems incomprehensible or irrelevant. We cannot cancel out their bewilderment by proclaiming: "Not what we say is important but what the Scripture says" or "the question is, 'who is Christ himself?' " All our central words, such as "salvation," "Christ," "church," and "Scripture," have a much more contextual shape and focus than we are aware of. Conversely, it cuts no ice either when Third World theologians regard our Western contextualization of the gospel as a (capitalistic, imperialistic, socially uncritical) corruption, and their own as a true, or even *the* true, interpretation of the gospel.

Now that we have discovered the contextuality of *all* dogmatics, we can go in two directions. We can welcome the fact because it breaks the overpowering influence of *one* type of contextuality and wherever possible promotes the practice in ever more self-conscious ways and in more and more places in the world, in order that "the manifold wisdom of God" (Eph. 3:10) may in time become more manifest. But we can also make an effort to promote the theology — in every geographic area and of course primarily in our own — that transcends its contextual limitation by also appropriating the truths that have been developed in other cultural contexts.

The first option commends itself because theology aims to serve the believer, the church, and the world. But it is simply the case that one can never serve all believers, the whole church, and the entire world. One can be fruitful only by addressing the church life and cultural climate in which one shares personally. That is how love of neighbor is best served in theology. We hardly need to confront each other with that dimension, however, because we can never expect to be able to bypass ourselves and our situation. The idea is rather that we need to be conscious of the limits of this approach to the gospel. Before we know it we think that this approach is the best — if not the only good one. From that point it is only one step to the dominance of the context over the message. Whoever regards the Christ of the West as too inward, too white, too masculine, and too conformist runs the risk of casting out the devil with the help of Beelzebub by developing a cosmic, a black, a feminine, a proletarian, a revolutionary (etc.) Christology. The result is that in theology we then get divisions such as are described in 1 Corinthians 1; and Paul's question, "Is there more than one Christ?" (J. B. Phillips) becomes even more applicable to our way of theologizing than was the case earlier.

Therefore, if we do not wish to divide the body of Christ in regional sectors, we must take the second option. This option is a Christian imperative because there is only one Lord, one Spirit, one faith, one hope, one body (Eph. 4:3-6). To believe the gospel is (*eo ipso*) to transcend one's own given social context. This option is also an academic imperative. Truths in physics, history, ethics, and also theology either have universal validity or they are not truths. The revelation of God as well as the scientific enterprise both assume the unity of humankind and seek to establish it. Whatever evangelical truth is discovered and developed from within one context applies to all contexts. We in the West cannot bypass discoveries made in India concerning the cosmic Christ, or those made in Latin America concerning Jesus as the partisan of the poor, as if those truths belonged in another cultural and political climate. We depend in life on the communion of the saints — and in dogmatics also. That fact does not exclude criticism and discussion; for these are based on the very assumption that one takes seriously the truth-claims of the other. Dogmatics is therefore universal or it is not dogmatics.

But how can we square that claim with the contextuality that is also demanded? One who proceeds from contextuality as his main platform will not be able to fit universal validity into it. But one who proceeds from universal validity will naturally be driven to contextuality as a consequence. For the universally valid core is the love of the Lord who seeks out the lost sheep where it is situated in its estrangement. And that situation differs each time — socially, culturally, and psychologically. Therefore, the universal is pointed toward the particular without losing itself in it. It is precisely in that pointed address, in which human beings are grasped where they are, that they are redemptively brought toward perspectives that transcend their context in a way that broadens and relativizes. This applies to the sermon, the church's teaching, and pastoral care. In dogmatics it means that contextual blueprints coming from different angles and corners always have to converge without having to coincide. And by leading people to the one Lord they lead at the same time, by way of complement, to other blueprints and open the way toward understanding and loving others in their different situations.

Six

THE FOUNDATIONS OF DOGMATICS

6.1 IS DOGMATICS A BUILDING WITH FOUNDATIONS?

If in the two concluding chapters we want to discuss the content of dogmatics more deliberately and directly than was possible earlier, we must make a twofold division. We shall follow the distinction between a building and its foundations. Of course that is only an image. Within the discipline itself a distinction is made between foundational and material dogmatics or between the prolegomena and dogmatics proper. There are other such names. In some cases, hardly any distinction is made; in others, for instance at Roman Catholic institutions of theology, there are frequently two distinct chairs of theology, one of which is designated that of "foundational theology."

Just what can such a distinction refer to, and does it make sense to make it? We recall that earlier we talked about the foundations on which theologizing must rest (chaps. 2 and 3). Then we referred to source-experiences, conduits, building materials, ancillary disciplines. But now that we are about to speak of the building and its structure, some of these matters must be brought up again, and that not only insofar as they concern us as the presuppositions of dogmatics, but also as fundamental elements within dogmatics itself. But can dogmatics have something like foundations? Is not God, who reveals himself and is known to us by faith, its one and only foundation? In the order of being, that is self-evidently the case. But in the order of knowing we use the word "foundation" to refer to something else. Then the question is whether in dogmatics, analogously to other disciplines, we have to deal with fixed starting points, organizing frameworks, ever-returning points of orientation: formalized summary concepts that impart to the subdivisions of the field the necessary cohesion and consistency and can therefore also serve as courts of appeal and norms, as our thinking proceeds. No academic discipline — which, in the nature of the case, aims to make the data clear and coherent — can do without such a fundamental conceptual framework.

In dogmatics these "fundamentalia" were, and are, not always given such conscious and separate attention. Dogmatics is often treated along the lines of the Apostles' Creed. One then plunges directly into material dogmatics, beginning with God and the creation. That happens especially when in the circle for which the work is intended the Christian faith is viewed as secure and more or less self-evident. But when the fellowship of the faithful is itself divided about the nature and definition of revealed redemption, or when the adherents of the Christian faith find themselves involved in sharp dialogue with the non-Christian world, the need to have an epistemological justification may be strongly felt. An example of the first was the conflict between Reformation and counter-Reformation scholastic theology (especially in the sixteenth and seventeenth centuries). An example of the second is the dialogue that has been taking place in our secularized Western culture for two centuries now. In both periods the search was, and is, for comprehensive and normative concepts that must impart the power of logical persuasiveness to the whole as a reflection of the *one* style of the *one* self-revealing God.

Since the Reformation, Roman Catholic theology posited the church, or its doctrine of the one, infallible church, as the foundation on which the whole of dogmatics had to be built. The Reformation, on its part, chose as foundation the Bible, or its doctrine of the sufficient, infallible Scriptures, and hence developed dogmatics on the basis of "proof-texts" from the Bible.

Later, both of these authorities were more or less replaced as foundation by others — revelation, the history of salvation, the Spirit, religion, or the anthropological structure — as so many perspectival points of reference or centers in terms of which salvation could be surveyed in its totality. We shall discuss each of these foundations, briefly, more or less in historical sequence.

6.2 THE CHURCH

There is genuine plausibility in treating dogmatics within the framework of the church. For whatever dogmatics may claim for itself, it is always an expression of the Christian faith as it is held within a certain ecclesiastical fellowship. That is the common denominator of everything that is treated. Hence this centralizing point of entry has played a dominant role not only in Roman Catholic dogmatics but also in a number of Protestant works: in the case of Schleiermacher, in "ethical" theology, and also in Karl Barth who took his stance within the event of the proclamation of the Word and called his work *Church Dogmatics*.

But its most extensive and consistent use occurs in classic counter-Reformation theology. At its genesis stands the three-volume work of the Italian Jesuit and cardinal Robert Bellarmine, *Disputationes de controversiis christianae fidei adversus huius temporis haereticos* (1586 – 1593), which was reprinted more than a hundred times in a century and a half. He demonstrated that the four attributes that the Apostles' Creed ascribes to the church — unity, holiness, apostolicity, and catholicity — apply exactly and exclusively to the church of Rome. The Bible, on the other hand, has an authority that is derived from the authority of the church. The Bible is the church's gift to us, and the church has determined its authority and canon. In succeeding centuries a similar apologetic-polemic treatment of ecclesiology in Roman Catholic manuals would preface the remainder as prolegomenon. First, it was demonstrated that there exists an infallible church; this was followed by an exposition of the faith. This scheme is not completely gone today but the number of those who follow it began to shrink around 1930 and has become smaller since the Second Vatican Council.

Why has this form of doing foundational theology receded so strongly? There are a number of reasons; first, we have become distrustful toward the ontological worth of so-called logically conclusive arguments. Since the nineteenth century, with its tendency in its theological method to orient itself to biology and to think "organically," many Roman Catholic theologians believe that this apologetic logic bypasses, and must bypass, the essence of the church as "the mystery of redemption." Another reason for distrust of this apologetic scheme is that it hardly leaves room for putting critical questions, from within the Bible or the Fathers, to the existing church and its hierarchy, or for trying to promote a further development of church doctrine. It is a form of foundational theology that confirms one side of an argument and leads to fossilization. It was only when many scholars abandoned it that a renewed florescence of dogmatics could occur in the Roman Catholic Church.

6.3 SCRIPTURE

Just as Bellarmine and his followers posited the infallible church as foundational to the whole of redemptive truth, so Lutheran and Reformed scholastic theologians posited the infallible Scriptures as foundational to their dogmatics. The first person to do this on a broad systematic basis was Amandus Polanus à Polansdorf, son-in-law of Theodore Beza and dogmatician at Basel, who wrote his *Syntagma theologiae christianae* in 1609. He was followed immediately by the Lutheran Johann Gerhard with his *Loci theologici* (1610) and a short time later by the very popular *Leiden Synopsis* (1624). These works start out with a broad exposition of the doctrine concerning the infallible Holy Scriptures. Here, too, four attributes are usually central: authority, necessity, sufficiency, and clarity. On these the infallibility of Scripture rests.

But this Protestant foundation soon began to show cracks (even before the Roman Catholic foundation). There was too much material in the Bible that was not in harmony with the concept of infallibility ascribed to it. The first thing that caused trouble was uncertainty with regard to the original form of the text. If no uniform and infallible text has been handed down we do not have an infallible Scripture in our hands. There were scholars who doubted the reliability of the Masoretic Text of the Old Testament and regarded its late vocalization as decidedly unreliable. To close this hole the Zürich "Formula Consensus," appealing to Romans 3:2, in 1675 declared both the traditional vowels and the Masoretic consonants to be inspired. But their effort failed: the emerging historical-critical method, with its sensitivity to the human side of Scripture, blasted one hole after another in this foundation.

The fact that the authority of Scripture as foundation and formal principle in orthodox Protestant dogmatics proved so tenacious is due especially to the spiritual authority with which the Bible forces itself upon us as content and standard of the faith. But Calvin already understood that Scripture is much more to be regarded as instrument than as foundation. Over against the Roman Catholic doctrine that the authority of Scripture is derived from the authority of the church, Calvin taught that, from the human point of view, the internal testimony of the Holy Spirit is its foundation (*Institutes* I.7). This doctrine, added to his personalized understanding of Scripture ("God in person speaks in it", I.7.4) and his doctrine, applied especially in his commentaries, of the "accommodation" of God in his address to puny man, could lead to a much less rigorous doctrine of the authority of Scripture. This line of thought was later adapted by H. Bavinck, who on the one hand based Scripture as foundation on revelation, of which it is the precipitate, and on the other on the witness of the Spirit (*Gereformeerde Dogmatiek I,* chaps. II and III). Others again, as we shall see, more radically made these two foci of authority into the foundation of faith.

6.4 REVELATION

Although the dogmaticians of orthodox Protestantism (in the broad sense) did not, after the rise of Bible criticism, abandon Scripture as the foundation of dogmatics, they could not possibly use it anymore as a collection of infallible proof-texts. For from start to finish the Bible is a series of human testimonies. What unites these testimonies is their reference to *one* God who has made himself known in very distinct encounters and of whom the witnesses, each in his own way, testify. Their words, then, refer to an event or process of events that lies behind and above their testimony. We are accustomed to designate as *revelation* that nexus of events that take place in ever new and distinct encounters. It is understandable that many theologians used the word *revelation* to refer to the foundation on which they built their systems of reflection. In using this word it was not their intent to give up Scripture as foundation; their purpose was rather to liberate it from the procrustean bed of a theory of inspiration that cannot do justice to its humanness and diversity. But that is not to deny that a shift is taking place here: a foundation is laid beneath a foundation. Bavinck rooted his "external principle" in the concept of revelation and, just before he had reached the halfway point in his chapter, abruptly forged the link with Scripture. Others are more radical; as, for instance, Helmut Thielicke who in *The Evangelical Faith* (vol. 2, *The Doctrine of God and of Christ* [Eerdmans, 1977]) subsumed the entire work of God and Christ under this concept as, respectively, the "origin" and "form of revelation." One senses the difficulty: this abstract concept in which, moreover, the central notion of salvation is lacking, lends itself only to limited use.

Many, therefore, feel the need to replace it with a more concrete notion. It is natural, then, to declare Christ to be the foundation of dogmatics: "For no other foundation can any one lay than that which is laid, which is Jesus Christ" (1 Cor. 3:11). That tendency exists especially in the Lutheran tradition; for Luther himself, remember, only wished to acknowledge as having authority "that which promotes Christ" (*was Christum treibet*). But that seems more simple and convincing than it is. In the light of this standard Luther spoke in rather derogatory terms about the Epistle of James; and that was because for him Christ and "justification by faith" were identical and he could not find this equation in James. But in this way "Christ," rather than being a foundation, can become a restrictive ideology. The same thing happens if we take as our foundation a synoptic Jesus, one that has been smoothed and fitted by historical criticism. One cannot detach the name "Christ" from its prehistory in the Old Testament, nor from the proclamation that eyewitnesses built upon his death and resurrection. But, having said that, we are virtually back to Scripture as our foundation.

The most impressive methodological concentration on Christ is to be found, in my opinion, in Barth. Although one can clearly sense in this christological concentration the influence of his Lutheran teacher Wilhelm Hermann, Barth manages to escape the danger of a too narrow focus by proceeding from "the Word of God in its threefold form," that is: (1) the incarnate Word; (2) the written Word; (3) the preached Word. Thus the foundations of revelation, Scripture, and church are grasped simultaneously in a single movement (*Church Dogmatics,* I/1, 4). And in the end this revelational movement is anchored in the doctrine of the Trinity (I/1, 8-12). Barth knew, better than many of his predecessors, how to escape from the danger of an abstract Christ-principle. But against this concentration, to which all the biblical testimonies were related and made subordinate either as expectation (O.T.) or as recollection (N.T.), objections were raised. The question was: Is the entire content of revelation enclosed in Christ as the crucified and risen one?

It is not strange that others, beginning already in the nineteenth century, introduced into the concept of revelation not a concentration but a historic extension, by making the concept "salvation history" fundamental. Christ, after all, rather than exhausting Scripture, is in turn end point, starting point, and center of a long covenantal history that God first experienced with Israel and then undertakes with all humankind. And the Bible, from Genesis 1 to Revelation 22, is primarily and principally a history book. The New Testament scholar Oscar Cullmann, in *Salvation in History* (Harper & Row, 1967) has elaborated this as the all-embracing point of view. In dogmatics this was done even more radically by Wolfhart Pannenberg, for example, in *Revelation as History* (trans. David Granskou [Macmillan, 1968]). His concern is not only with the biblical history of redemption, but with the history of the world.

But there are objections to be registered also against using the concept of history as foundation. For history means change: shifts and turns. For a thing to be foundational it needs to be a constant, a suprahistorical element, that expresses itself in our history and *makes* history there. Even then history by itself has no revelational power; that power will always have to come from the Word that illumines the many-sided and multivalent course of events. Again we are dependent on revelation as Scripture.

In our time, too, these positions are widely current, and in Roman Catholic theology as well. But they seldom or never occur in pure form. Typical examples of systematic theologians who take as their starting point the christocentric Word-event are Walter Kreck, *Grundfragen der Dogmatik* (1970), and E. J. Beker and J. M. Hasselaar, *Wegen en Kruispunten in de dogmatiek* (1978), with a strong emphasis on the scriptural form. A much heavier emphasis on history as component in revelation is laid in the multivolume postconciliar dogmatic series *Mysterium Salutis,* with the subtitle "Outline of Redemptive-Historical Dogmatics" (1968ff.)* and H. Berkhof, *Christian Faith: An Introduction to the Study of the Faith* (Eerdmans, 1979).

6.5 THE SPIRIT

In 6.3 and 6.4 we have sketched briefly the development of and changes in the Reformation principle of Scripture to the present. Now we must return to the sixteenth and seventeenth centuries in which arose, almost simultaneously with the Reformation, the so-called spiritualistic movements, which acknowledged as their only foundation the inward testimony of the illuminating Spirit. In the eyes of the adherents of these movements, Protestant orthodoxy had reduced Scripture to a "paper pope," a purely external locus of authority. A favorite text of these movements was, and still is, "it is the Spirit himself bearing witness with our spirit that we are children of God" (Rom. 8:16).

A favorite expression of this, especially among Quakers, was "the inner Light." Robert Barclay, a Quaker, wrote *An Apology for the true Christian Divinity* (1676), a study of the faith constructed on the foundation of this inner light. This classic work has a clearly christocentric beginning but there Christ

---

*See esp. the volume *Revelation* by Heinrich Fries (Herder and Herder, 1969). — Trans.

is "the true light that enlightens every man coming into the world" (John 1:9), a light that has its most powerful concentration in Jesus but can also be known as the universal power of love outside of him.

The same train of thought, though with a different set of concepts, occurs in the work of the Leiden theologian J. H. Scholten, who wrote *De leer der Hervormde Kerk in hare grond-beginselen* ("Fundamentals of the Teaching of the Reformed Church," 1848). In this work he proceeds from two foundations, the doctrine concerning Holy Scripture as the formal principle, and predestination or "the confession of God's absolute sovereignty in the natural and moral world" as the material principle. In Scholten's thought the first principle culminates in the authority of the reason and conscience of the individual; the second in a deterministic and, simultaneously, optimistic monism.

So, making the testimony of the Spirit in our hearts our sole foundation, we also end up wrong. As an isolated principle it is too subjective and too individualistic for us to arrive at stable and universally valid structures in dogmatics. One can, in the main, go in two directions with it. Like Calvin, one can tie the Spirit tightly to Christ and Scripture, so that he derives his norm and content from these sources. Or, one can detach the Spirit from the specific historic revelation embodied in the Bible and treat him as the fundamental principle of all religiosity and humanity in the world. We have seen how Barclay and Scholten began with the first and ended up with the second.

But in liberal Protestantism, which leans strongly toward a spiritualistic foundation in dogmatics, there repeatedly also arises the opposing movement: that from a universal and natural religiosity toward a more christocentric one. A familiar example of this in the Netherlands is G. J. Heering, *Geloof en Openbaring* (vol. 1, 1935; vol. 2, 1937). Without this countermovement a dogmatics built on a spiritualistic foundation loses its intellectual structure and community-forming power.

Conversely, it is also true that a dogmatics in which one does not honor the unique work of the Spirit alongside the Word easily leads to authoritarian objectivism. In this connection it is quite significant that it was Karl Barth who repeatedly said that after completing his christocentric dogmatics he would dearly have liked to start on a new plan, this time proceeding from the Spirit and his work in shaping us.

6.6 MAN

The order we followed in the material of 6.2 to 6.5 is to some extent a historical one: first the Roman Catholic way of laying a foundation, followed by the orthodox Protestant one in its classic forms, then in its modern forms, and finally the liberal Protestant one. We saw the latter moving from a specifically pneumatological to a universal anthropological foundation — by which process it seemed that dogmatics would dissolve itself. The actual course of events was otherwise.

After Descartes, and particularly after Kant, it was man himself, in our secularizing culture, who began to play the pivotal role as the lord of nature, as legislator of his world, and as judge of the authority-claims of the Christian faith. Schleiermacher was the first theologian to realize fully the implications of this for dogmatics. Anyone wishing, with its help, to gain a hearing for the Christian faith in contemporary culture will from now on have to involve man, to whom revelation is addressed, as a fundamental datum in his reflections.

That could be done, of course, on a basis of radical spiritualism; then the human spirit itself becomes the place where God reveals himself. A small circle of left-wing liberals continues to think in that direction. But then so little remains of the basic notions of the Christian faith that most dogmaticians prefer to assign a more modest role to man as factor in the process of revelation. But in the work of many a scholar that role is still formidable enough. One must bear in mind that the word *man* or *human* refers not only to an anthropological substructure but more generally to a point of departure in the earthly environment to which man belongs and which gives him the experience by which he is nurtured.

If we put it this way it becomes clear at once that the fundamental role of man was consciously or unconsciously taken into account long before the present secularization in dogmatics. In the thirteenth century, when the first wave of secularization washed over Western Europe, Thomas Aquinas answered it by picturing the supernatural life as the completion of a natural life that he sketched in Aristotelian terms. It is for this reason that even today the majority of the theologians who take man as their starting point can be found in the Roman Catholic tradition. One of the greatest and most pronounced representatives of this type was Karl Rahner (1904 – 1984), who locates the core of humanness in the human drive toward self-transcendence, toward "transcendentality"; Rahner pictures the Christian faith as the (only) answer that corresponds to the radicality of this drive.

In Protestantism it was only after the Enlightenment that theologians began to treat man as a fundamental point of entry. Schleiermacher began with it by proceeding from "the human consciousness of being absolutely dependent" as the core of existence. The most impressive modern example of this approach is Paul Tillich (1886 – 1965). His three-part *Systematic Theology* is consistently built up on the method of "correlation," by which he means that to be human in its deepest essence is never to cease asking questions, and that God's revelation is intended as an answer to these questions.

Just as Aquinas defined man in Aristotelian terms, so also have all these modern theologians conceived of man by drawing from a (usually contemporary) philosophy: Schleiermacher takes his point of departure in idealism, Tillich in the existentialism of Heidegger, others in that of Jaspers, still others in the principle of hope as defined by Ernst Bloch, or in the encounter with the Other or the other (Lévinas). Biological constructs of man (Gehlen, Lorenz), or general scientific constructs (the "process philosophy" of Whitehead), or socioeconomic constructs (Marx, Marcuse) play such a widespread fundamental role. Dogmaticians as a rule hardly ever or never take over such conceptions *in toto*; usually they are tailored to fit elements in the biblical message.

A manifest advantage of dogmatics done on such a foundation is the high level of intelligibility and expressiveness that is gained as a result. When the apostle Paul had to address the intellectual Greeks at Athens, he began by taking his position in Stoic patterns of thought (Acts 17:22-29), going so far as to quote with approval one of their poets. He could do this because the entire Bible witnesses to a God who searches for and captures individuals in the historic and psychological places in which they are situated, in order subsequently to establish a two-sided covenant of Word and response with each person. There is reason to assume that for many people within and also outside the Christian church, especially the young and the educated, this modern point of entry became a point of access to the gospel.

But the limits and dangers of this method are no less manifest. Almost automatically it brings with it a harmonious view of the relationship between man and God, between experience and revelation. For this method only works if man and his experience offer the blueprint that largely establishes the dimensions of the building. The difficulty is that the gospel with its themes of sin, deliverance from above, the leading of the Spirit, justification, and conversion by no means positions itself toward man in a harmonious, accommodating way. Upon closer scrutiny these designs often show, for that matter, that their anthropology is from the start more or less tailored, as we called it earlier, toward the evangelical view of sin, grace, and renewal. But to that same extent its claims of universal validity are undermined.

Man by himself cannot be the foundation and starting point of dogmatics. The gospel is brought to us as a "happening" from within history. As such it cannot be construed in advance. In relation to our general concepts it is contingent and discontinuous. It is an encounter and, as such, like all genuine encounters, unpredictable in nature and effect. We cannot get this encounter in our sights from within ourselves or from what we think we know about our deepest being. By this approach we give ourselves far too much weight and give God, as initiative-taker, far too little.

It was especially Karl Barth who for that reason wanted nothing to do with this point of entry. He posited that if one does not start with God one will never end with him — only with an enlarged projection of oneself. His attack on every foundation other than that which has been laid, namely Christ, was so radical that it looked as if it would be the death-blow to any anthropological starting point in dogmatics. Still, after Barth such starting points came back forcefully to the center of the theological arena. In my opinion, this must be explained in terms of the ever-increasing estrangement between the church's message and modern man. The battle over the relationship between revelation and experience is more intense than ever as I write these words (1982). We have repeatedly touched upon it in preceding sections (see esp. 3.4, 5.2, and 5.4). It is not necessary to take it up again explicitly at this point. But no one can make progress in dogmatics without taking a position on this issue.

Nevertheless, as we now draw up the balance sheet for this chapter in a concluding section, we shall have to broach the problem (tangentially) one more time.

6.7 COMBINATION AND VERIFICATION

The rapid survey we have made of the starting points that have been attempted in dogmatics until now has taught us, in any case, that none of these can serve as foundation and norm in abstraction from the others. Over and over one is forced to go from one to the other. Leaving aside for the moment the anthropological point of entry (6.6), because of its special character (it is the only foundation not derived from revelation itself), we even have to say of the other four that they apparently form a unit and that not one of them can be had by itself. No matter at which station we enter the train of dogmatics,* we are bound to make a stop at the remaining three. Apparently, the train travels around by way of four stations. Thus we ride around the open center field of material dogmatics. Dogmatics is not a road that takes us from a fundamental simplicity to more complex problems and insights. Everything proceeds from everything else and everything presupposes everything else and nothing outside of it is prior to it except for God himself and his Word, which "comes to pass" in our midst.

This is not a circle that permits itself to be broken into by theological thought. One can only jump into mid-circle. Dog-

---

*N.B. Toward the end of 4.8, dogmatics was the central station, the place of trans-shipment, for the products of other disciplines; here we have an "intramural" metaphor and dogmatics has become a train stopping at various stations and moving on a circular route. — Trans.

matics, after all, mirrors a faith that enters the revelational circle not by logical argument but by an act of surrender. That jump may appear to be irrational to the outsider, but for the believer it is the very opposite and for the dogmatician it justifies itself by the web of connections that he discovers one by one.

It is precisely in that coherence, and not in a unilateral choice of one of these four foundations, that the norm for evaluating the truth content of a given dogmatic pronouncement is given. The more clearly the pronouncement is supported by those four pillars, the more tenable it is. Dogmaticians are comparable to children sitting on the floor around a box of toy building blocks, which is missing the instructions. One child uses the blocks to build a railway station, another a castle, a third a church, and so on. But each one has a few blocks left over. Each critically points his finger at the blocks for which the others had no room, but cannot use all of them himself, either. Extending the image, we can say that that dogmatician has penetrated his subject matter most deeply who, approaching his object systematically from a fourfold combination of entry points, has the least number of building blocks left, that is, has neglected the least number of points of view. Every dogmatician continually has to measure his work in terms of the requirements of these foundations; and by their discussions dogmaticians should help each other in that process.

In the course of this discussion we have brought to light an internal criterion of truth to be used in theologizing. In our day, however, many people are much more interested in an external criterion, one that flows from the general human consciousness of truth. Can dogmatics "tolerate inquiry" (Kuitert) and, if so, how? Are its results more or less verifiable by the outsider as well? The picture of the leap into a circle arouses suspicion. It seems that by means of it dogmatics has withdrawn from dialogue in the sphere of culture and scholarship — with a claim to possessing secret information ("revelation"). It is for this reason that in the last two decades, with their strongly empirical or even empiricistic character, there are questions concerning the "verification" or "falsification" of dogmatic statements (the terminology is that of the philosopher Popper); that is to say, the question is whether there are generally valid standards by which their accuracy or inaccuracy can be measured. Having said this, we are clearly back at the fifth point of entry: man and the human awareness of truth.

The concepts of verification and falsification are very useful in the world of mathematical and scientific research. But that usefulness is limited in the humanities. The higher the levels of human freedom and active agency, the more complex the field of study is, and the larger the element of subjectivity. The picture of the toy building blocks comes to mind again. In that context one avoids the word *verification* and refers rather to *plausibility* or (especially in Roman Catholic theology) *insightfulness*. The question is: is even that attainable, when we think of the objections to an anthropological foundation, which we considered in 6.6? Or when we call to mind the image of the circle? Are not faith and dogmatics based on an irrational leap, a *sacrificium intellectus*?

But if the movement into the circle of faith must be called a "leap," then that word is appropriate for a variety of discoveries that we make in the course of our lives, such as the discovery of what is love or beauty. We cannot talk anyone into an appreciation of them. And anyone experiencing them needs no further argument. The breadth and depth of our humanity can be measured by the number of such illuminations, which come to us from without and touch our egos at the core. Under these circumstances even the word "leap" proves inadequate. What happens is not a decision we take but an experience that comes over us and that we cannot, and usually do not want to, resist. Afterward we often come up with a rational justification for the experience, for instance, because the event has widened our awareness, enriched our humanity, integrated a number of preceding experiences, and motivated us to undertake a new ethical practice. But all these "reasons" do not say anything to a person who is unfamiliar with the precipitating event.

Or is that untrue? Do they say something at least? Such renewals and broadening experiences can also affect the outsider. But the outsider cannot take them over by means of rational argument and conviction based on it. But they can remove irrelevant intellectual and emotional resistances. The dogmatician who knows the time in which and for which he practices his discipline must be alert to these possibilities. Next to the four foundations that bound the revelational process, man who is the addressee of this process will never be out of the dogmatician's mind and so will play a fundamental role in his thinking. But because of the nature of the subject one does not, in this domain of knowledge any more than in many others, get beyond a certain measure of insightfulness. Whether the spark of illumination will jump from one mind to another is not something one can control with argumentation. In the name "Holy Spirit" we give expression to the nonmanipulability as well as to the possibility of this happening. Perhaps also the dogmatician will serve this process of events. But even then we may expect more from his exposition of the subject than from his argumentation about the subject. "Even" Schleiermacher knew that "the presentation of Christianity is at the same time its defense." For that reason we now conclude our introduction with a glance at the subject matter itself, so-called material dogmatics.

Seven

THE BUILDING ITSELF

7.1 THE DIVISIONS OF DOGMATICS

If dogmatics can be compared with a building, then one can and must also discuss the arrangement of its parts. In the nature of the case every dogmatics is divided in a series of chapters, each of which relates to a specific division, such as sin, reconciliation, or the church. In Roman Catholic theology there is talk of "tractates," in classic Protestant theology, of "loci." That division can, of course, take place in a variety of ways; we intend to return to the subject later. What needs to be stressed first of all, however, is that the arrangement of the material by itself is of secondary importance. It is of secondary importance, first, because the question arises only in the case of a complete work of dogmatics. But most dogmatic work is presented in the form of monographs. It is secondary, also, because in recent decades many dogmatic insights come wrapped in themes that are offerings from other quarters, as, for example, liberation, feminism, or Second and Third World criticism of Western theology. The titles thus mention "A theology of. . . ." Personal dogmatic insights are then developed obliquely or at the end. Even if one were to call this genre "pre-dogmatic," one must not overlook the fact that many starts or stimuli for a new way of doing theology are offered in this indirect manner. Third (and this is the main argument), material dogmatics can be compared with a circle in exactly the same way as formal dogmatics: after all, they relate to the same subject matter. One can enter it at every point because everything is connected with everything else.

Still, the arrangement of the material is not so arbitrary a thing as may seem from the preceding. The subject matter treated in dogmatics to a certain extent brings its own limited possibilities of division. Since the subject matter concerns the "happenings" between God and man, one can start either on the side of God or on the side of man. A number of noteworthy treatises begin with the effect of God's redemptive revelation in the life of man. Augustine, in his *Enchiridion,* developed the content of faith within the framework of the concepts of faith, hope, and love. Melanchthon, in the first printing of his *Loci communes,* started with the relation between man and the law and then showed how grace redeems us from it. The arrangement of the Heidelberg Catechism is very original: from within the need for comfort in life and death it treats the entire contents of the faith under the perspectives of misery, redemption, and gratitude. Schleiermacher described the Christian faith consistently as "the explication of the religious self-consciousness." The school of Ritschl tended to return to the scheme of the young Melanchthon. So Horst Stephan proceeds from faith, its ground and its content (*Glaubenslehre,* 1920). But the more orthodox theologian Martin Kähler develops all the loci under the title "Von dem Gegenstande des Rechtfertigungsglaubens" ("Concerning the object of faith in justification") in *Die Wissenschaft der Christlichen Lehre* (1883).

Nevertheless, only a minority has applied this principle of division. The majority opted for a starting point in God, in his being and his revelation. This probably relates also to the fact that authors, especially in dogmatics books and booklets written for nontheologians, tended to orient themselves to the widely known and used Apostles' Creed. That would automatically lead to a trinitarian setup: God, creation, Christ, Spirit, redemption, consummation. Most works, the most classic ones among them, have this setup; this includes such Roman Catholic works as Aquinas's *Summa theologica* or M. J. Scheeben's *The Mysteries of Christianity* (E.T., Herder, 1946) as well as the classic reformational works, from Calvin's *Institutes* to Barth's *Church Dogmatics,* and the more liberal, such as the stringently trinitarian three-volume *Systematic Theology* by Paul Tillich.

Even with this commonality of arrangement there is variation enough. Thus, between the doctrine of God and Christology, Aquinas treats not only the anthropology of creation and sin (as is usual) but also, at great length, the doctrine of the natural and the supernatural virtues (II.1, 2), and then demonstrates (in III) how we arrive at the sanctification and perfection of life through Christ and the operation of the sacraments. A totally different deviation from well-trodden paths occurs in Barth's volumes on reconciliation (II/1, 2, and 3), in which he thrice addresses, each time from a different perspective, the person and work of Christ, then sin, next the church, and finally the matter of personal appropriation.

The most customary division, following the treatment of the foundations in the introductory part (often called Prolegomena), is the following: being and attributes of God; creation; man and sin; the natures (divine and human), states (humiliation and exaltation), and offices (prophet, priest, and king) of Christ; atonement and reconciliation, justification and sanctification; the church and its attributes; the consummation. The order of individual and church also may be reversed. In recent years "the life of Jesus" is often treated more deliberately, and the relation between the church and the world comes more to the fore.

Proceeding from this scheme we shall, in the following sections, broach a number of problems that always, or particularly in our time, get special attention. There is one theme we shall not touch; that is the relation between revelation and experience, a theme that came up in the preceding chapter on the foundations of dogmatics and several times before that (3.4, 5.2, 6.6, 6.7). What *is* touched upon is only a selection made by the author. That selection is subjective, of course, but I hope not arbitrary. It is simply the case that at certain times certain parts of, and problematics in, dogmatics occupy center stage while others remain in the shadows. But that can change tomorrow. Experience teaches that we repeatedly return to themes, and even to solutions, that we had prematurely labeled as "dated" or "obsolete." These are words we had better avoid in dogmatics. But it is true that changes in culture, faith, church, and scholarship tend, in dogmatics, to affect especially certain loci or tracts, and it is in these areas that most of the influential scholarship, studies that "change boundary lines," takes place. By offering rapid surveys of five such areas, I hope to enable my readers to classify, more or less, a variety of recent or soon-to-appear dogmatics studies.

7.2 GOD

For centuries, amid numerous changes of culture and intellectual fashion, things have been relatively quiet in the doctrine concerning God. For God, as compared with a restless world, was immutability itself. That fact was mirrored, right through the division of times and the splitting of churches, in the relative immutability of the *locus de Deo*. The Apologists and the early Fathers had already laid down the fundamental lines for the doctrine of God. In the face of the Hellenistic, pluriform world of religions and of many — and often limited and capricious — gods, they confessed (leaning on the monotheistic philosophy of that time) the one immutable God, who was elevated far above the disturbances and suffering of the human world. They taught, as did Plato, that "God has no attributes," and in the Middle Ages theologians adopted Aristotle's definition of deity: "the first to set in motion without itself being set in motion by anything" (*to proton kinoun akinèton*). This God is almighty, omnipresent, omniscient, unchanging, infinite, incomprehensible. For centuries these omni-, un-, and in-, words dominated the doctrine of God. They gave expression to both the exaltedness and the firmness that people sought to find in God.

Still, theologians were aware, of course, that the point of gravity in the biblical pronouncements concerning God lies elsewhere. Central to these pronouncements is his wrath and his mercy, and there is mention even of his repentance. In these pronouncements are repeated references to changes in God; in them, his Word becomes a human being and he journeys with his Spirit through the world. Usually, theologians said that all this had reference to God-in-his-relationship-to-us, not to God-in-himself. But, one must ask, does God present himself in his relationship to us in a way that is different from what he is in himself? Augustine and the young Luther tried to understand God much more in terms of his relationship to us, his condescension and immanence. But they were the exceptions. The main line of thought remained the one we find back in the Belgic Confession, for example, where Article 1 offers a definition of God by means of abstract omni- and in- words, and it is only from Article 17 onward that the love of God in Christ comes to be central — without, however, allowing this confession to modify the definition of God given in Article 1. This one-sided image of God is still present in the hearts, or at least in the unconscious, of numerous Christians and non-Christians: God, the rigid ruler far above us, the all-seeing eye glaring balefully down on us.

German Idealism constructed another image of God: the immanent One, the Spirit of our spirit, who dwells and works in history. Theology refused to accept the pantheistic implications of this view, but began in the nineteenth century, supported by this philosophy, to stress God's immanence and kinship with man in virtue of our freedom, our moral consciousness, and our conscience — so much so that the deity of God now threatened to be absorbed and exhausted by the humanity of man. After the petrification of the God-image in the footsteps of Aristotle, its vaporization in the footsteps of Hegel now threatened; or, following Kant, God became a projection of our ethical consciousness. It was then that Karl Barth forcefully reached back to the deity of God, to his sovereignty and transcendence. Still, he did not fall back on the earlier one-sided position. God, in Barth, is consistently defined by his reconciling incarnation in Christ. From all eternity God is a communicative God, an "Event," to be defined as "One who loves in freedom." The splendid explication of this conception in *Church Dogmatics* II/1 for a long time seemed to be the last word.

In time, however, many dogmaticians felt impelled to advance in the direction Barth had indicated, but further than Barth had gone. For if God is a communicative God who, in virtue of who he is, involves himself in the lives and sufferings of his people, to the point of the incarnation of the Word and the outpouring of the Spirit, must we then not say that God takes part in history, that he shares in our suffering, and that by his deliverances among us he is also enriched himself? And can this be so for any other reason than that he has an everlasting history of communication within himself and the capacity for suffering? Must not the rigid traditional doctrine of the Trinity be filled and formed in terms of these insights? And must there not be a thorough review especially of the attributes of omnipotence and immutability? In Scripture they hardly play a role. God's omnipotence is still hidden, on the way toward becoming visible. In Scripture God's immutability is called his faithfulness, expressing itself in his unceasingly active choice in favor of his estranged creatures, who inspire him to devise ever-changing means to restore them to himself. Apart from the internal problematics of the doctrine of God, external factors also clearly play a role in this radical review: in our time we are witnessing enormous changes in the world and we refuse to believe, in the manner of the old theology, that God stands outside and above them. It was probably Bonhoeffer, in his *Letters and Papers from Prison* (Macmillan, 1967; reprt. 1972), who was the first to realize what was at the point of happening in the doctrine of God. His notes on the powerlessness of God became fundamental for the development that followed.

In this development little can be done with Tillich's doctrine of God, in which God is defined as "Being itself." That does not mean, however, that theologians are totally averse to receiving help from the side of philosophy. In Germany, for example, Jüngel and Pannenberg lean heavily on Hegel. In the Anglo-Saxon world there is a strong orientation to the process philosophy of Whitehead, who saw God not only as the basis but also as the unpredictable outcome of the process of becoming in which the world and the human race are caught up, an idea on which Hartshorne, Cobb, Ogden, Williams, and Pittenger based their further embroideries as theologians. The German group, among whom also Moltmann may be counted, anchors this doctrine of God in a speculative theory of the Trinity. The Anglo-Saxon group comes close to being a new form of natural theology. A wide range of diversity proves to be possible between, say, the orthodox Protestant Jürgen Moltmann with *The Crucified God* (E.T., Harper & Row, 1974), and the liberal Catholic

Pohier with *Quand je dis Dieu* ("When I say God," 1977). But what unites them all is the attempt to link God with human suffering and vice versa without divinizing the suffering in the process. Somewhat to the side of this development is the manner in which feminist theology seeks to purge the God-image of its patriarchal-authoritarian traits by giving prominence to the maternal and feminine in God. The underlying purpose in all of this is to think through the "humanity of God" — a phrase that Barth already coined.

It is not now possible to indicate a common theological denominator or travel route. That which unites the different groups is the negative: a common aversion to God as the great Outsider. Much quoted is the definition of Whitehead, who described God as "the fellow-sufferer who understands." In this connection one does wonder in what respect God is superior to, or has an advantage over, the world. Without a plus-factor God's deity drops away and hence his power to redeem this world from its state of guilt and suffering. In other words, God's immanence is not relevant to us without his transcendence, just as his transcendence is not a healing thing without his immanence. The effort to think through both aspects on a conjoined basis is for the moment, to my knowledge, most clearly undertaken by Eberhard Jüngel in his *God as the Mystery of the World* (trans. Darrell Guder [Eerdmans, 1983]).

7.3 THE WORLD AND MAN

In classic dogmatics these subjects are generally treated under the headings of "creation" and "fall." There are good reasons why at this point we have chosen other words. The "world," in this dogmatics, remained wedged between God as its creator, on whom it was totally dependent, and the sin of man, by which it was totally estranged from God. Occasional positive pronouncements about the world as it now "runs and reels" were subsumed under the heading of "preservation" or "providence" but were marginal even there. The "world" was especially the world of sinful man and so the world as it lies "in the power of the evil one" (1 John 5:19). In this connection there was always a clear difference between Roman Catholic and Protestant theology. In the first, the fall into sin was the loss of supernatural gifts, while the natural life remained largely intact; in the second, the fall into sin was the rebellion of man by which he cut his ties with God and so retained only a "remnant" of the image of God.

It was Barth who, immediately after World War II, astonished both friend and foe with his extensive and positive doctrine of creation (*Church Dogmatics* III/1) and shortly afterward with his matching doctrine of man as creature (III/2). This second volume especially, with its striking emphasis on man's co-humanity as centered in the man-woman relationship, proved a big help in shaping a Christian attitude toward the then incipient construction of a welfare state. This work is still of fundamental importance. It ushered in a period, which continues into the present, in which the world and man are no longer primarily considered and described theologically from the perspective of sin but from that of creation.

Barth, of course, was not the sole cause of this new emphasis. The principal cause lay in the explosive expansion of our world-experience after the Second World War. The development of technology, the awakening of the Third World, the rise of the social sciences, medical discoveries and inventions, television, the reduction of the work week, the pill, social tourism, and so forth have made of us very different people than were our ancestors and grandparents. We experience all these things as an enormous expansion of our humanity. We cannot possibly subsume all of them under the heading of the doctrine of sin (the misuse of them is, of course, a different story).

Roman Catholic theology has less difficulty relating to these experiences than that of Protestantism. "The theology of earthly realities," "Theology of the world," "A theology of culture," are typical titles of Roman Catholic books. The constitution *Gaudium et Spes* ("The Church in the Modern World") of the Second Vatican Council is a good specimen of this genre. Protestant literature, as a rule, is more reserved. It tends to view the world and man in it more in their unredeemed ambivalence. Books that develop a theology of secularization usually come from the side of Protestantism. In Catholic theology, what the world and man in it need is "completion" and "perfection"; in Protestant theology it is "reconciliation" and "salvation." Roman Catholic thought often impresses the Protestant as too optimistic and facile; conversely, the Roman Catholic views Protestant thought as too darkly pessimistic and preoccupied with sin. But both are an address, be it with different emphases, to the same cultural climate. And together they currently face a number of new problems. We shall refer to a few of them.

1. The relation of man to his *Umwelt* (environment). Did we get our anthropology too one-sidedly from Genesis 1 (man as crown and lord of creation)? Is that not partly a product of idealistic philosophy? Must we not view man more as having arisen from matter, as we see it depicted in Genesis 2? Did we do justice to the discoveries of Darwin and Freud? Especially, have we, following Marx, really gained insight into the socioeconomic conditioning of our thought and action? Add to this the environmental crisis of recent years, which raises anew the question whether man can rightly be called the lord of nature and should not rather be called the keeper and administrator of the earth. For that matter, is man the central focus of creation, as he fancies himself to be? What if, at some time in the future, other and possibly more gifted spiritual beings are discovered in this universe with its astronomical dimensions in time and space? Is the Copernican revolution an ongoing thing? And what, then, is the response of the Christian faith?

2. The relation of man to his *social contexts*. For centuries society appeared to be a relatively static whole. Now we view it as part of an entire world in process of becoming. Can theology continue to speak of established "creational ordinances" such as marriage, family, labor, authority? An assortment of fixed behavior patterns from the past is perhaps not instituted by God but thrust upon us by socioeconomic or other forces. Or do certain ontological structures, given with the creation and rooted in the benevolent will of God, really exist, and are they such that we cannot ignore them with impunity? If that is the case, then can we tell the one from the other with the help of theological criteria?

3. The relation of man to *sin*. It is much harder today than it used to be to draw a line of demarcation between that which is created and that which is sinful in us. For example, is aggres-

sion sin? But without a certain amount of aggression a human being cannot come to full development. Or is self-development evil and only self-denial good? But anyone who neglects to develop the self is unable to sacrifice it to God and neighbor. Is homosexuality sin? But for the homosexual it is heterosexuality that is contrary to nature. And so we can continue the line of questions and examples. At the same time we know of sin as an omnipresent destructive force. But where does the good creation end and sin begin? And can we then still speak of *original* sin? Can that which has been inherited ever constitute a personal sin? And if it can, how can it?

4. The relation of man to *God*. All the questions we have touched upon come to a grand focus in this fourth dimension. The notion of God as the all-powerful Creator on whom we are totally dependent seems in recent decades to have lost much ground. All sorts of things that Lord's Day 10 of the Heidelberg Catechism ascribed to God's all-powerful providence, such as "food and drink, health and sickness, riches and poverty," appear or prove now to belong largely to the domain of human power and responsibility. The fact that man was created as ruler of the world after the image of God himself (Gen. 1:26-28) therefore has implications that are much greater than we thought for centuries. But what in this grand interplay of factors is, then, the peculiar role of God? Is he still able to preserve his creation, now that man has in the last few years managed to get the power to destroy it? No wonder that in the last few years there has been fresh reflection on the doctrine of providence! That cannot be done in isolation from the broader context of creation and redemption: Does God, in redemption, confirm this creation — or does he deliberately leave it behind in order to attain something higher?

7.4 ISRAEL

In this heading we are referring first of all and principally to the Old Testament in its relation to the New. But because the Old Testament relates to a history between God and one people, and because the history of that people has continued to this day,

the question of the scope of the subject matter we are here dealing with extends far beyond the boundaries of the Old Testament.

As a rule, there is no explicit treatment in dogmatics of the
question of the status of this first and largest part of the Bible.
In 7.1 we mentioned that many dogmatics were oriented in their
structure to the Apostles' Creed. That creed, and the later longer
confessions as well, ignores God's way with Israel in the Old
Testament. The Apostles' Creed leaps, as it were, from the creation to Christ. In dogmatic theologies the doctrine of sin is
treated in between these two, but the question concerning the
content and meaning of the revelation to Israel is not answered.
And when it is summarily broached the answer comes back
quickly: the Old Testament foretells the coming of Christ. Especially in the churches and theologies of the catholic type the
Old Testament is explained "allegorically" (as a reference to a
higher spiritual truth) or "typologically" (as a reference to the
coming fulfillment in Christ). This is different in the Lutheran
tradition; there the Old Testament is especially the book of the
law that kills, just as the New is the book of grace. Calvin, too,
credited the Old Testament with a significance of its own but
one that is more in harmony with that of the New. In the *Institutes* (II.6-11) he speaks of the unity of the two testaments
as it concerns the *substantia* that is contained in the one covenant, while the difference lies only in a different *administratio*.
Still, this observation did not lead, in Reformed confessions and
dogmatic theologies, to a description of the significance of the
Old Testament, barring the one notable exception of the Scottish
Confession, Chapter V.

In the Netherlands, where many Jewish fugitives found shel-
ter over the years, "the ancient covenant people" were treated
with respect. In the seventeenth century, Christian theologians
invited rabbis to teach them Hebrew; in the nineteenth century,
under the influence of the *Reveil* (Revival), a vigorous Jewish
mission came into being. Both led to special interest in the Old
Testament and the Jewish interpretation of it. This interest was
deepened and broadened in the twentieth century as a result of
Jewish persecutions. In theology, all this might not have had
any effect if in 1956 the work of Miskotte, *When the Gods are
Silent* (E.T., Harper & Row, 1967), concerning the meaning of

the Old Testament, had not appeared. This book became foundational for later development in the Netherlands, especially as a result of its strong emphasis on the "advantage" of the Old Testament, which, so much more than the New, brings ordinary life on earth to bear on the relationship with God. As elements of such a "favorable balance" Miskotte mentions, among other things, the primitive element, the narrative, law, suffering, poverty, eros, and politics. In connection with what we noted in 7.3 about the force with which the world in its horizontality presented itself after World War II, also in theology, it is understandable that the book exerted great influence on theology and the pulpit in the Netherlands and still does so today. By saying this we are also asserting that here we have a typically Dutch dogmatic theme. For although Miskotte's work was translated into German and English, it has not had the same far-reaching influence in other countries. That influence must certainly be explained also in terms of the long Reformed and Jewish traditions in the Netherlands.

Still, Miskotte's intent was not to offer a well-weighed and complete theology of the covenant with Israel. His interest lay in the peculiar new accents in teaching and proclamation that the Old Testament makes available. But in the same year, 1956, A. A. van Ruler published *The Christian Church and the Old Testament* (E.T., Eerdmans, 1972), in which he presented the Old Testament as really the higher revelation that can only be reached by way of the detour of the New: the "humanity" of the kingdom of God on earth has to be reached by way of expiation for sin. The Old Testament does not itself speak of Christ but is directed toward the eschaton. More even than in Miskotte, the Old Testament is here understood as a message-by-itself. A later design for a locus on the Old Testament was offered by the present author in his *Christian Faith* (Eerdmans, 1979) in the chapter entitled "Israel." He embeds it, together with the New Testament, in a long covenant history. In that setting Israel is the "experimental farm" in which the failure of man as covenant-partner becomes manifest. Thus the Old Testament cries out for the true covenant-partner, Christ.

Speaking generally, these days so much emphasis is accorded to the positive content and independence of the Old Testament that one wonders why Jesus still had to come. Continuing Barth's line of thought concerning the Old Testament as "adequate prefiguration" of the prophecy of Jesus Christ and hence as "complete Messianic prophecy" (*Church Dogmatics,* IV/3, 1, p. 65; [but cf. the German original, *K.D.* IV/3, 1, p. 71 — Trans.]) many scholars locate the center of Scripture in the Torah and view Jesus as the obedient Torah-scholar and the true fulfiller of the law. This procedure just has to lead to an undervaluation of everything in Jesus that places him over against or above Moses. Others go still further and try to locate the hermeneutic key for the understanding of the Old Testament in Mishnah and Talmud, not in Jesus, while still others look for it in the covenant reciprocity between God and man — as modern liberal Judaism views it. In the theology of liberation the hermeneutic center is located in the Exodus of the exploited from Egypt (as the house of bondage), and the entire Old Testament (together with the New) is regarded as explication and realization of that redemptive event.

But all these positions raise profound questions, which still await a clear definition and answer. First, there is the question concerning the "positive balance," the genuinely new element of the New Testament, and, in the light of it, "the negative balance" or "lack" of the Old, and then the question of the relationship between them. Also, there is the question concerning the difference between the hermeneutic of the Old Testament in the New and that of the Talmud. The question of Paul's legitimacy as interpreter of the Old Testament needs to be stated thoroughly and anew. Does the center of the Old Testament lie in the Torah or in the prophets? How are the Exodus and the Exile related, and how the wilderness and the promised land — as useful or nonuseful points of entry and as normative or as nonnormative structures of faith? Finally, the question needs to be answered whether the Old Testament, though "spiritualized," can be legitimately assimilated by the Christian, or if it has to be reserved for Israel — and then in the full materiality of its people, land, prosperity, and so forth. Regrettably, one needs to say that with regard to these questions we are dogmatically still in a "pre" phase in which more is posited than thought through — one reason why there is no dialogue between representatives of the different views.

With this last question we have gone far beyond the boundaries of the Old Testament. After all, Israel is not just a "figure" in the pre-Christian history of salvation; it is also a religious, national, and political reality in the present. Paul's thought in Romans (chaps. 9 – 11) also prompts the dogmatician, when thinking of Israel, to view past, present, and future in one perspective. The first question, then, is whether, theologically, one must view the Israel of the Bible in one continuous historical line with the Jews of today. If one believes he should, he then faces the next question, that is, whether the church has replaced pre-Christian Israel in God's plan of redemption (the so-called substitution theory). If one denies this, he then faces the question of whether Judaism and the church represent two equally valid ways of salvation. Stated differently: Do the Jews still stand in a peculiar covenant relationship with the God of the fathers? If so, in what ways does that relationship then become concrete? In a religion of fidelity to the Torah and a synagogal structure? In the refusal to assimilate with the Gentile world? In survival despite an unimaginable history of suffering? In the return to the land and in the creation of the state of Israel?

Added to this, following Hitler's extermination camps, is a series of other, very heavy questions: What does God's silence in Auschwitz mean for such a covenant relationship? And what does this genocidal murder mean to the church, which for centuries wrote off Israel and so became an accomplice? And what does this unutterable suffering mean for faith in God's providence?

All the questions summed up here are also, in whole or in part, dogmatic questions. The answers to them have implications for the doctrine of God, Christology, and ecclesiology.

After what I remarked about the unique role which the Netherlands played in reflection on questions concerning Israel, it is odd and disappointing to state now that there has been little systematic theological reflection on the present-day Jewish phenomenon and the church's relation to it. It seems that many theologians shrink from the task. Continuing reflection could perhaps tie in with the embattled publication of the Hervormd

Synod: *"Israel—volk, land, staat"* ("Israel: its people, land, and state"). Another source is E. Flesseman–van Leer: *Met de Schrift tussen Kerk en Jodendom* (1982) [a selection of Bible studies and articles on the relationship between the church and the Jews, ed. H. Berkhof]. On the theme of "God after Auschwitz" there has been more theological reflection in North America and Germany than in the Netherlands. For a study of this theme a consideration of Jewish theology is unavoidable (E. Berkovits and E. L. Fackenheim *contra* I. Maybaum and R. L. Rubinstein). For a comprehensive survey of names and problems, see S. Schoon, *Christelijke presentie in de joodse staat* (1982), chap. IV.

7.5 CHRIST

The status of questions relating to Christology is very different from the status of those concerning the Old Testament and Israel. Christological questions are currently posed around the world and are equally relevant, be it not always in the same way, in Latin America and in Germany, as much in Roman Catholic as in Protestant theology and also among Anglicans— witness the intense controversy over the book *The Myth of God Incarnate* [Westminster Press, 1978].

The deepest cause of this seems to me to lie in the shift that occurred during the fifties and sixties in the climate of scholarship and culture when the pendulum swung (once again) from a more idealistic approach to reality from above, from within the thinking and willing spirit, to a more empirical one from below, from within the material world. In Christology the contrast between spirit and matter shifts to the distinction in Christ between "very God" and "very man." Where do we start and where should the emphasis be? Must we construct a Christology "from above" or one "from below"?

This twofold approach can already be found in the New Testament. The Synoptic Gospels begin with Jesus' baptism or birth and concentrate on his earthly life, culminating in his resurrection. This approach is also present in some early creeds (e.g., Rom. 1:3-4), or in summaries of the earliest preaching of Christ (e.g., Acts 2:22-24; 3:13-26; 4:10-12; 5:30-32). Over against it stands the approach of John's Gospel, which takes its point of departure in eternity, starting with the Word that was in the beginning and viewing Jesus' earthly life as surrounded by an aura of glory — the glory of his preexistence and postexistence. Paul, who concentrates on Christ's death and resurrection, can be found one moment on this line and the next on the other.

In the early church one encounters Christologies from above and from below, depending in part on whether the influence of Plato or that of Aristotle prevailed. But the Johannine "model" repeatedly gained the upper hand and was viewed for centuries as *the* orthodox Christology. Still, even within this model the tensions remained, as appears from the profound difference between the Christologies of Luther and Calvin. It seemed that the Council of Chalcedon (451), with its formula of "two natures in one person," "without mixture, change, division, or separation," had devised the solution, but the formula did not answer the question whether the one person is divine or human. Most theologians said the first was true and so were forced to speak of an "impersonal human nature"; but there were also ever those who, with an eye to the synoptic story, did not think this solution was real and were afraid that in this manner the real humanity of Jesus would not be recognized. It is for that reason that christological discussions never came to a halt. In our time there is the additional factor that the language of Chalcedon has become unintelligible for many, but the synoptic story of Jesus and his radical love and self-denial continue to enthral numerous people inside and outside the churches.

Not surprisingly, in the last twenty years there appeared a stream of christological studies that sought to approach the mystery of Christ "from below." In this connection we can regard Wolfhart Pannenberg's *Jesus — God and Man* (Westminster Press, 1968; 2d ed. 1982) as foundational. He starts out, broadly, with the results of scholarly research into "the historical Jesus" and his relationships to God and to the future. But in what follows it turns out that he sees those unique relationships as, so to speak, the earthly underside of a supra-earthly mystery: the eternal trinitarian relationship between the Father and the Son. So the principle "from below" here has only a methodological significance; in the order of knowing the movement is from below to the top, but in the order of being the order is reversed. The same is true in the Christologies of Rahner (*A New Christology*, Karl Rahner and Wilhelm Thusing [Crossroad, 1980]), of Moltmann (*The Crucified God* [Harper & Row, 1974]), and "even" of Schillebeeckx (as is apparent from the unfinished conclusion of *Jesus: An Experiment in Christology* [Crossroad, 1979; Random House, 1981]). Since in these works "humanness" and the capacity for suffering is accorded to the trinitarian Godhead himself, this leads to bold speculations concerning the Trinity, especially in Moltmann.

Others are not willing to make any distinction, or at least want to make much less distinction, between the order of knowing and the order of being. To them Jesus is the true Son of God precisely because he is human, the true covenant-partner of God, the eschatological man, in whose image we may be renewed. It is in this line that we find Schoonenberg, *The Christ* (Herder and Herder, 1971); Flesseman–van Leer, *A Faith for Today* (Assoc. of Baptist Professors of Religion, 1980); Berkhof, *Christian Faith* (Eerdmans, 1979, pp. 31-37); and Küng, *On Being a Christian* (Doubleday, 1976). In their thinking the Trinity is not the name for an intradivine mystery but a description of what has happened and is happening between God and men in revelation and covenant.

Still others seek to position themselves, regarding both the order of knowing and that of being, as closely as possible to Chalcedon. That is the case with Beker and Hasselaar (Vol. 3, *Wegen en Kruispunten in de dogmatiek*, 1981), who follow the line of Barth. The most significant example of this on the Catholic side is Walter Kasper, *Jesus the Christ* (Paulist Press, 1976). This book is at the same time a proof of the extent to which classical doctrine can be enriched with biblical-theological and modern insights.

Conversely, from the developing trend of thought among the more radical theologians "from below" it is clear that for them the new humanity embodied in Christ rests on an act "from above." Something is happening here below — a man among men — that can only be interpreted from above. More "classical" theologians, on the other hand, applying the historical-critical method, now give much more space to the life of the earthly Jesus than used to be the case.

But the points of entry remain more or less opposite and they determine, and restrict, what it is one gets into his line of vision, christologically speaking. One who starts out from a trinitarian eternity and the incarnation is bound to leave somewhat in the shadows the life of Jesus, his genuine humanity and intense struggles, and his obedience as Son of the Father. But one who starts out with all this, though able to present the cross as the self-offering of an obedient martyr, will have a much harder time picturing it as an act of reconciliation from the side of God, and probably leave underexposed the resurrection of Jesus as an act of divine intervention.

It could be that the subject matter itself is the reason why we cannot rise above this back-and-forth movement between the two perspectival approaches in Christology. But before long we may perhaps come up with the conceptual categories by which our points of entry will be broadened and our fields of vision may move toward greater overlap. As long as this is not the case, those who wish to become familiar with the problematics of Christology will do well first to measure the distance between them, for example, by a comparison between Pannenberg's *Jesus — God and Man* and John A. T. Robinson's *The Human Face of God* (1973; Westminster Press, 1979).

7.6 THE SPIRIT

This section has the same heading as 6.5, which may serve to bring out once again the fact that our division between formal and material dogmatics, or between the foundations and the building, is at best a distinction within one structural whole in which the several themes have fluid boundaries. In 6.5 our focus was the Spirit as the principle by which we know the whole of revelation. It became apparent, then, that the Spirit does not lend himself well for that purpose because he derives his "content" from the contexts in which he operates. He cannot function in fundamental dogmatics unless we first reflect on his being and work in material dogmatics. And that, for centuries, is precisely what has not been done, at least not adequately, within the churchly orthodoxies. Special attention to the Holy Spirit was more or less suspect. Such attention was typically something that marked heretics — or that created them. In the Roman Catholic Church there was no need for it because the Spirit was regarded as the soul, the animating interior, of the church. Under these circumstances there is no need for a separate pneumatology in addition to ecclesiology. In the Reformation the Spirit is eclipsed by the saving means of the (written or proclaimed) Word and is, in addition, the self-evident ground of regeneration, justification, and sanctification. In the independent churches, and in Pietism and Methodism, the Spirit comes more to the fore, but then as the origin of individual faith; there, too, because the impulse to do systematic theology is not strong as a rule, little comes of theological reflection on the subject. And in the leading German theology of the nineteenth century, a theology in which the word *Geist* (Spirit) tended to occur often, the influence of philosophical idealism was so strong that the divine and the human spirits could merge. An end to this trend came with the shock of World War I and Barth's *Römerbrief* (E.T., *The Epistle to the Romans* [Oxford Univ. Press, 1933; 1968]). But Barth's strong concentration on Christ and the sense of living "between the times" offered no clear answer to the question concerning the presence of God here and now. Spirit, in this theology, meant his nonmanipulability, sovereignty, and vertical operation as "Event."

It was during and after World War II that a number of theologians became aware of the pneumatological vacuum in which they found themselves and began to seek ways to give theological expression to the uniqueness of the Spirit and his work after, and next to, that of Christ. This pneumatological interest, remarkably enough, went furthest in the Netherlands. It started with Noordmans who, though spiritually akin to Barth, at an early stage registered his objections to Barth's then-current vertical-incidental pneumatology: "in this theology the church gets to be somewhat like a haunted house in which God puts in sudden appearances at unexpected moments." Fundamental for our theme is Noordmans' *Gestalte en Geest* ("Form and Spirit"; 1954), in which the Spirit is presented as creating ever new configurations of life and leaving earlier ones behind. In addition, the graphic figure of the synoptic Jesus must be left behind to make room for the interpretation of Christ in the Spirit as we find it especially in Paul. Noordmans, by his daring intellectual thrusts, tended to anticipate later insights.

More daring still was the pneumatology that van Ruler developed in a variety of articles. In him we find a strong contrapuntal relationship between Christ and the Spirit, which, in his grand essay on the "Structural differences between the Christological and Pneumatological point of view" (1961),* almost becomes a contradiction: after man has been suppressed in the atoning work of Christ, the Spirit comes to raise him up to autonomy and cooperation with God. While van Ruler thus positioned himself squarely over against Barth, for whom the Spirit is precisely the One to represent Christ to us, Berkhof attempted in *The Doctrine of the Holy Spirit* (John Knox, 1964), by extending Barth's line of thought, to track down the uniqueness of the Holy Spirit: the Spirit is the name given to the presence of the exalted Lord whose activity, after that of the earthly Jesus, is now addressed to the entire inhabited world. Among non-Dutch theologians special mention must be made of Tillich, who gave us the third and last volume of his *Systematic Theology* (1963; part IV: "Life and the Spirit"); in this more liberal pneumatology, the uniqueness of the Spirit of Christ is related, as "healing presence," to the entire range of the "ambiguities" of our personal and social lives.

The flash flood of the "God-is-dead" theology washed over these and other developments in the second half of the decade of the sixties. But when the tide turned, there remained a particularly strong theological interest in the activity of God as Spirit in the present. The search for new roads to travel went on in two directions:

1. *The social-ethical "school."* Here the presence of the Spirit is sought in the praxis of politics; in advocacy on behalf of the oppressed and exploited; in the commitment to liberation and, if necessary, revolution; in the willingness to suffer as disciples of Jesus. Such Catholic theologians as Gutiérrez, Metz,

---

*I have translated the Dutch title; the lecture, as far as I know, is not available in English translation. — Trans.

and Schillebeeckx, and such Protestant theologians as Goll-
witzer, Moltmann, Ter Schegget, and Sölle, think in this direction, be it with considerable differences among them. Still, from
a pneumatological point of view, the movement has not been
very fruitful, because in this school of thought man with his
activity and responsibility has been made so central that a strong
emphasis on the Spirit as inspiration, norm, and motive for this
praxis is experienced more as a hindrance than a help—the idea
being that this would reduce the sense of human responsibility.
The movement seems still to be too strongly under the spell of
a (semi-) Pelagian mode of thought.

2. *The charismatic "school."* This arose as a movement in
the established churches in the same period. Here the Spirit,
together with his special gifts, was made entirely central. Initially the emphasis lay on glossolalia and healing, later also on
the gift of prophecy. To the extent that this trend grew into a
revival movement, there was also more theological reflection on
it. People began to reflect on concepts like "being filled," "baptism with the Holy Spirit," "the Spirit as earnest." On the Catholic side we refer especially to the American Simon Tugwell and
the German Heribert Mühlen. The festschrift for Schillebeeckx,
Leven uit de Geest ("Living by the Spirit," 1974), which contains contributions from non-Catholics as well, offers evidence
in several of its essays of a new pneumatological search. Reference must also be made here to the thorough, ecumenical sym-
posium edited by Heitmann and Mühlen, *Erfahrung und
Theologie des Heiligen Geistes* ("Experience and Theology of
the Holy Spirit"), primarily written by German theologians. The
literature produced by American Protestants is already immense.
The variations in this type of thought have hardly been mapped
out, to say nothing of their having led to a kind of consensus by
way of internal dialogue.

It is not entirely out of bounds to suppose that both schools,
the social-ethical and the charismatic, may produce too little in
the way of pneumatology, the first because of its emphasis on
man and his work, the second because of its reduction of the
Spirit to his work in the inner man of the individual.

For that reason a rapprochement at this time of both schools,
ecclesiastically and theologically, could perhaps be the most sig-

nificant phenomenon. This rapprochement is taking place mainly in Latin American theology, in which liberation theologians, conservative evangelicals, and leaders of charismatic movements are beginning to discover each other, the first being in search of a "spirituality of combat," the others being in search of the "worldly" forms of the Spirit. I am familiar with this phenomenon especially via the ecumenist Emilio Castro and the conservative evangelical Orlando Costas. It would seem that the key words "fulfillment" and "liberation" are in process of converging. Pneumatological research and reflection may possibly await us in precisely this direction.

In this connection it remains for me to call attention to (the recurrently neglected) *English* and especially *Anglican* theology. In his impressive Bampton Lectures *God as Spirit* (Clarendon Press, 1977), G. W. H. Lampe offered a fresh statement of the Spiritualism by which he understood Christ in terms of the universal Spirit and not vice versa. The reverse is done by the well-known missiologist John Taylor in *The Go-Between God* (1972; Oxford Univ. Press, 1979) in which the work of the Spirit is explored over a wide range and in which there is much material that can help us in bringing about the convergence to which we referred in the previous paragraph.

7.7 OTHER THEMES

Toward the end of 7.1, I remarked that the selection of themes in 7.2-6 would, of course, be subjective but, hopefully, not arbitrary. To banish the second and reduce the first possibility I believe it is well for me to refer briefly to significant themes that did not come up for discussion in the preceding sections.

1. *The doctrine of the atonement* did not arise; that is, especially the question concerning the redemptive significance of Jesus' suffering and death and its theological formulation did not come up. In Dutch Protestantism, this question repeatedly sparks the most heated discussion: Is God reconciled with man or is it only man who is reconciled with God? Does that reconciliation take place entirely outside of us, in Christ, or by way of an event in ourselves, or in the moves we initiate to bring

about reconciliation among people? Again and again the old difference between Anselm's "objective" doctrine of atonement and Abelard's "subjective" one flares up. Especially Dorothee Sölle, with her book *Christ the Representative* (E.T., Fortress Press, 1967), and Herman Wiersinga in his dissertation *De verzoening in de theologische discussie,* * both of them theological blueprints of a more subjective type, added fuel to this smouldering fire. Two pastoral letters were issued by Reformed churches: *De tussenmuur weggetrokken* ("The removal of the wall of partition"; Hervormd, 1967), and *Verzoening met God en met mensen* ("Reconciliation with God and with men"; Gereformeerd, 1977). It does not look as if a dogmatic consensus has been reached. In Roman Catholic theology this problem hardly plays a role, perhaps because it is concealed behind the controversy concerning the sacrifice in the Eucharist.

2. *The doctrine of the personal appropriation of salvation* was developed especially in the Reformation and the so-called Nearer Reformation [a seventeenth-century Puritan-Pietist movement in the Netherlands]. In a few seminaries and theological schools it occupies a large place in the theological curriculum. One can hardly speak of a present-day development of it, however, except in respect of controversies on matters of detail rooted in the tradition, controversies still understood by only a few people. Within the freer forms of theological practice interest in these themes is very small. The situation is different in the case of a variety of modern instances of experience-theology; but this theology is far removed from the semantic field of tradition, and prefers to speak about the saving change that takes place in man in terms of deliverance, emancipation, elevation, and the like. With these terms one runs the danger of not giving adequate expression to Christian salvation in the fullness of its depth and scope. The attractiveness of Hinduism and Buddhism to so many younger people in the "Christian" West is symptomatic of a large vacuum in reflection upon those realities which used to be called rebirth, conversion, surrender, justification, and sanctification. What we are waiting for is a

---

* "Verzoening" stands for both atonement and reconciliation, an ambiguity that makes it hard to translate this title. — Trans.

revaluation — one which if not acceptable is at least intelligible to contemporary man — of the grand words about human renewal that come down to us from the New Testament and the Christian tradition.

3. *The doctrine of the church* or *ecclesiology* has really always been a preoccupation of theology. It is simply the case that dogmatics is rooted in the church and aims to serve it. But for that very reason the positions and ambitions of the dogmaticians tend to vary a lot. For a while it seemed they were moving in this area toward a certain convergence — witness, for example, the ecclesiologies of Barth, Berkouwer, and Küng, as well as the Faith and Order report *One Lord One Baptism* (1960). But under the increasing pressure of secularization and no less of pluralism in the churches, it seems to us that this triumph was claimed too soon and that it is much harder for us today than it was a quarter of a century ago to form a picture of the church that is realistic as well as normative and does not immediately fall prey to ecclesiastical polarization. Still, in our churchly actions we cannot operate without some orientation and direction. But whoever ventures to construct a blueprint will need insight not only into the unity and diversity of New Testament ecclesiologies but also into the modern sociology of institutions. Currently it would appear that the solution to the large questions of the authority, offices, and structure of the church is being sought more in a free-church direction, where there is more room for plurality, functionality, and personal "enfranchisement." But no one should be surprised if before long the cultural winds will again begin to blow more in a high-church direction. However this may be, the dogmatician will have to do more than proceed with the wind at his back.

A necessary and wholesome counterweight is provided by ecumenical dialogue on age-old controversies, like that conducted under the auspices of "Faith and Order." Particularly the so-called B.E.M. report of the Lima conference (1982) with its startling consensus (of groups ranging from the Eastern Orthodox and Roman Catholic to the free-church tradition) concerning *Baptism, Eucharist and Ministry* will force dogmaticians everywhere to take a position.

4. *Eschatology.* It may appear that in the last few decades,

and certainly since the publication of Jürgen Moltmann's widely read *Theology of Hope* (E.T., Harper & Row, 1967), eschatology has in many different parts of the world been at the center of theological attention. But this attention was directed more to human hope as a dimension of the human spirit or of the Spirit— to use the jargon of the trade, more to the *spes qua* than to the *spes quae* [more to hope as a human activity by which we live than hope as the divine action that forms the content of our confidence]. The result was that this hope attached itself more to human activities than to divine promises. Often the focus in these treatises on hope was on the hopeful signs that we as believers have to erect in the present—hence on a part of ethics. Moltmann himself tried to counter the confusion of themes by distinguishing between *futurum* (the future that grows out of our actions) and *adventus* (the future that comes toward us from God's direction). Still, this distinction has hardly been given dogmatic elaboration. The result is that words like *hope, future, kingdom of God,* and so forth get an ambivalent and vague character. And in this same period, on the right wing of the church in large sections of the world, a realistic-apocalyptic preoccupation with doom, which has a large fundamentalist arsenal of Bible texts at its disposal, made its considerable impact. A sane dogmatics will not be able to share the answers given there; but we do need dogmaticians who understand the anxieties experienced and the question posed there, who will be able to devise better answers to those questions.